Meal Prep Bodybuilding Bible

Food science & nutrition for training big. Improve men's health, wellness, body, and sex drive. Fat-burning workout. Stretching exercises for men & 6-pack abs boost up

I0554748

Henrik Mulford

Table of Contents

Chapter 6 – What are the Best Practices for 6-pack and Abdominal Muscle Enhancement?

Conclusion

Introduction

Those who have ever seen a professional bodybuilder - or simply browsed through his Instagram feed – will probably be surprised to hear that his lean and muscular body is scored with a well-blended mixture of guided nutrition and exercise.

It is no secret that preparing meals is critical to staying on a perfect bodybuilding diet. As you probably know, when you're preparing healthy meals ahead, you're probably not going to run into any seemingly tasty unnecessary junk on the way home or when you're hungry after a workout.

Regardless of whether you're a decorated athlete, a nutritionist, or a bodybuilder, the bodybuilding meal preparation guide you're about to read is sure to change the game for you. By the way, some of the bodybuilding recipes that are contained in this guide are sure to make you drool. We're not going to be discussing just rice and chicken.

The Basics of Bodybuilding Nutrition

It's essential to clear the way by informing you that there's no one-size-fits-all nutrition plan in bodybuilding. This is obviously because not only are our bodies different, but our goals are also different. However, according to Paige Johnson, a nutrition therapist from The Diet Doc, most bodybuilding programs merge a low-calorie diet to a macro diet.

This idea is simple; counting calories requires you to track it and examine how much you eat each day. Calculating macronutrients (long for macros) implies that an exact percentage of total calories is derived from each of the 3 macronutrients, which are protein, fats, and carbohydrates.

Now, the precise macros percentage varies from one individual to another. However, most programs require carbohydrates at a high rate, a balanced protein percentage, and a tiny or reasonable fat percentage. This was put forth by Evan

Eaton, a nutritionist at Nutrishop.

So how is this calculated? That is the complicated part and why most athletes hire a nutritionist or a coach to help them figure out their caloric intake and macronutrient distribution. The coach or nutritionist also determines their plans for bodybuilding meal preparation. However, in this book, we'll be covering it all in easy-to-understand terms.

Most bodybuilders typically adhere to "cutting" and "bulking" periods. The cutting period is when they focus more on losing fat by cutting calories, while the bulking period is focused on building muscle (and eating extra calories in general). So since you're ready to prepare your own bodybuilding food and feed your stomach with good food, then get prepared to roll up your sleeves.
How to set your calorie and macro goals for bodybuilding meals

1. You need to discover the amount of energy you consume per day. The initial step to this is to figure out your daily energy intake. Anthony Balduzzi, who is the founder of The "Fit Father Project," described this are the close estimate of your daily caloric intake based on weight, height, activity level, and age.

2. You need to adjust according to whether you are bulking or cutting.

If the ambition is to cut down on fat and weight, then you need to eat fewer calories than your energy consumption figure. However, if you're trying to put on weight or muscle, you need to consume some more calories and then, you subtract or add 250 to 500 calories from or to your energy consumption figure. This will reveal your DTCI (daily target calorie intake).

3. You need to find out about your macro.
This will require some calculations to discover precisely how many grams of fats, carbs, and proteins you should eat on a daily basis. The following are some online tools that can help with this calculation:

- Katy Hearn Fit Macro Calculator
- IIFYM macro calculator
- BodyBuilding.com macro calculator
- A step-by-step guide to preparing a bodybuilding meal

The beginning of a bodybuilding meal plan is to understand the notion that you can eat any food as long as you do not exceed the required calories and achieve the ultimate ratio of 3 macros. This is why some people call this eating style" the flexible weight loss."

Know that preparing your food can greatly help you stick to your bodybuilding diet. This is because you preparing your meals makes it easier to stay on track and make good food choices if you can't cook. So does one prepare for this bodybuilding meal prep?

1. Get your tools

You should take advantage of tracking apps such as Lose It! And MyFitnessPal. With these, it becomes easier to choose and follow foods as they add up the macros and calories of each bodybuilding product. Also, these tools help you learn which foods contain proteins, carbs, proteins, and fats.

A kitchen scale is also helpful as it helps you measure food accurately compared to just portion sizes. Also, you should get some fixed cooking utensils for storing food.

2. Plan on buying food.

Next, on your meal prep preparation, you need to really be attentive to your grocery shopping. A close look at the categories, which are carbs, proteins, and fats, and plan for the 3 to 5 main foods you intend to eat in that week. Afterward, build a list of vegetables as they are your "go-to" foods, and these will be part of your lion's meal for the next week.

You should also ensure that when you choose the vegetables, you provide the colors varying as the different colors will represent minerals and vitamins and minerals. That way, you guard against nutrient deficiencies that prevent you from getting bored. Below are some ideas with which you can complete your bodybuilding meal menu.

- All-protein proteins: Chicken, beef, turkey, eggs, salmon, sardines, or canned tuna
- Proteins (Plant-based): Beans, quinoa, tempeh, tofu, textured vegetable protein, and vegan protein powder
- Healthy fats: nuts, avocado, Greek yogurt, coconut oil, seeds, and cheese
- Healthy Carbohydrates: Berry mixes, quinoa, sweet potatoes, rice, Oatmeal, Ezekiel Bread, Couscous
- Vegetables: Tomato, spinach, kale, paprika, cucumber, salad mix •
Spices: nutritional yeast, basil, hot sauce, balsamic vinaigrette, garlic, lemon, pepper, and salt

3. Prepare staple food.

Staying on track is vital to building the body you want, and that's only possible if you eat what you actually prepare. For this to work, you need to incorporate variety. So instead of making stews, roasts, and curries that lead to you eating precisely the same food for five days, prepare foods that can be combined in varying ways.

You can put your go-to protein with spices in the oven to fry. You can also go, fry the vegetables at the same time. Then use a hob or rice cooker for cooking carbs. Then you can steam all the vegetables you want to get your hands on and cook the eggs. After you've gotten everything cooked, you should store each ingredient in separate containers that you can grab quickly throughout the week.

4. Assemble meals.
Once all your food is cooked and stored in the fridge, all you have to do is take those dishes out, thereby combining them in multiple ways when eating. You can keep it simple by filling about half of the plate with any vegetable. You can fill a quarter of the container with protein; afterward, place a healthy carbohydrate on the last part. Note that if your macros are different, the doses will change; however, this is an excellent place to start.

One Day Ideas for BodyBuilding Meal Prep
First things first, no one's meal plan looks the same. The cooking ideas of person A and person B may not work with yours. However, they can be a great way to get your creative culinary juices flowing.

So for breakfast, you can make oatmeal overnight from cashew butter, dairy milk, flaxseed, chia seeds/pancakes from almond flour, hazelnut, olive oil, pureed fruit/spinach cheese, spinach, and breadcrumbs.
For lunch, you can pour one of your proteins into a side salad made of diced avocado, tomato, cucumber, salt, tomato, a pinch of lemon, and vinegar. You can also combine it with a carbohydrate. This could be sweet potato or canned salmon with Greek avocado. Yogurt and avocado mayonnaise can make for a quick, unbaked protein-rich meal.

For Dinner, you can mix a large salad cup with avocado, organic quinoa, then top with tofu, chicken, or tempeh. You may also combine similar ingredients into a burrito, sandwich wrap, or deconstructed burrito to turn it.
Now because I know how hard it can be when you're just starting, we are adding bodybuilding meal delivery services that can help you get started as soon as possible. So if you have, you tried making bodybuilding meals, but you just can't summarize it every week? Fortunately, there are proper organizations that can deliver ready-made meals based on your goals and diet. Below are such companies that give it right to your door.

- Handlebar kitchen
- FlexPro meals
- meal
- Meal icon
- Awesome Macros
- Fuel meals
- Eat Clean Bro
- Muscle Meals 2 Go

How to prepare a meal for bodybuilding

Since we're still discussing ideas that can help you get started quickly, let's talk about how you can make your entire week airtight in advance. Preparing a meal may seem like a complicated or daunting to-do on the outside, but we can break it down in stages to help you smooth out your diet.

Step 1 - Plan and Buy
An essential early note to yourself is that you will stick to the plan once you have prepared the weekly meals. Plain rice and grilled chicken is bodybuilders' bread and butter, but it may not be as delicious in the eighth part of the week. Buying in bulk is also usually cheaper - so figure out what you want to eat and buy it a lot. To achieve a balanced meal, Include a source of high-quality protein with each meal, add a source of carbohydrates, and make sure you also get fruits and vegetables.

Step 2 - Prepare it
Once you have arranged your grocery list, the next step is to move on to cooking. Make sure you choose foods and cooking methods that will last well for as many days as possible in storage. However, note that you have to be careful when using a lot of oil or sauces. This is because they may not sit well in a container containing protein or leafy vegetables.
A few helpful pro-tips for a culinary wave that is coming through your kitchen include first multitasking. You can fry chicken breast while steaming vegetables; you don't have to do things one at a time. Also, should you own a rice cooker, you can use it when everything else is warming up.

Secondly, organize yourself in advance as you can save lots of time in your kitchen if your kitchen is clean. So keep the knives sharp, the proteins cut, and the vegetable chopped before you start the oven.

Thirdly and perhaps one of the essential tips, make it fun. No need to enslave and struggle in silence. Preparing a meal can be the time to plan your workouts for the week, watch your favorite Netflix program, watch a good podcast, or even do a quick home workout while the food is in the oven or pot.

Step 3 - Measure twice and prepare once
Once you have put your culinary skills to work in the kitchen, bring out a food scale and a reliable calculator. If you pick up enough whole foods to distribute all your weekly meals, a simple calculation should make sure each dish has even amounts of protein, carbs, and vegetables.

Once everything is divided and packaged, it is helpful to record the total calories and distribution of macronutrients in each container, even if all meals are the same. Once you've cleaned up and your meals safely stored in the fridge or freezer, you're ready in a week.

Divide your food into several meal packages to ensure that each meal has healthy portions of protein, carbohydrates, fat, and calories.

Chapter 1 – Food Science and Nutrition for Bodybuilding

Generally, when people first hear of bodybuilding, their minds go straight into weightlifting and a whole lot of physical exercises. However, in time, they soon learn that a lot of building the right body has to do with diet. The purpose of a bodybuilding diet is for the formation of muscles and the reduction of body fat. It is geared towards the proper consumption of protein and carbohydrate-containing foods like pasta, cereal, wholemeal bread, and more. Obviously, there are variations here and there, but bodybuilding has plenty to do with what goes into your body at the core of it all.

So as to give you a proper understanding of nutrition as it relates to bodybuilding, let's go back to the origins. Many scholars share that bodybuilding diets originated from the ancient Greeks, whose gods -for instance, Achilles, Hercules, Apollo- were often depicted with well-chiseled bodies. Many people usually take this as a mere coincidence, but at the very least, it shows that the people who told the great Greek myths understood what a god must look like.

This led to ancient Greek societies imitating the ideology behind the right physical shape. The same desire for perfection is found in ancient Egypt and Rome. The modern era of bodybuilding began late in 19th century Europe. Eugen Sandow, the German powerhouse, is considered to be the first professional bodybuilder known. The man was featured in the 1893 World Columbian Exposition in Chicago for his strength.

This is a man who opened a chain of 20 weight training studios in England and also published a magazine containing diet tips. This renowned bodybuilder's diet was high in protein, calories, fats, and carbohydrates. So essentially, you can tell that bodybuilding is nothing new, and men have always understood the high importance that nutrition plays.

Typically, today, a bodybuilding diet contains from 2,500 to 5,500 calories daily for men, while for women, it ranges from 1,500 to 3,000 calories per day. Of course, these figures will depend on the type and level of exercise done. The protein, carbs, and fat ratio in the meal may also vary. While specific programs recommend 40% protein, 40% carbs, and 20% fats, others suggest a ratio of 40% protein, 30% carbs, and 30% fat. So that shows that there can be no one-size-fits-all on the matter.

Also, most bodybuilding diets comprise supplements and also protein powders. Unfortunately, in recent times, the focus of bodybuilding has shifted away from an emphasis on health to appearance at all costs. To achieve a much-hyped, better, and bigger body, many builders have invested a lot in nutritional, supplemental substances, and illegal use of steroids.

Obviously, all diets require an exercise routine spanning 3 to 7 days a week which usually comprises cardiovascular exercises and weight lifting. Note that your body burns
up to 50 calories per day for every pound of muscle you gain. With that, you know that adding 10 pounds of muscle can burn up to 500 extra calories every day. The precise diet and exercise routine may differ significantly and can be confusing, especially for people who are new to bodybuilding. No two people follow the same pattern regarding diet or exercise.

KEY TERMS for Basic nutrition for bodybuilding

- Amino Acids – certain organic acids which are components of a protein. •

Carbohydrates - An organic compound that is a vital source of energy in

foods

- Cholesterol - A solid compound that's in many foods and also present in the blood

- Epidemiologist - A scientist that studies disease and how it is transmitted.

- Glycemic Index (GI) - A way to classify carbohydrates based on their effect on blood sugar levels.

- Glycemic Load (GL) - A more in-depth categorization of how specific amounts of food affect blood sugar levels.

- Glycogen – This is a compound stored in the muscles and liver that can easily be converted to glucose energy.

- Insulin – This is a hormone responsible for regulating blood glucose levels.

- Monounsaturated fats are a kind of fat present in vegetable oils, e.g., peanut, olive, and rapeseed oils.

- Pancreas - The gastrointestinal tract responsible for regulating certain hormones, i.e., insulin.

- Polyunsaturated Fat - A kind of fat present in certain vegetable oils such as safflower, sunflower, and corn.

- Saturated Fat - A kind of fat that's common in meat products containing visible fat and dairy products.

- Trans fat is a kind of fat common in whole milk products, butter, pastries, fried foods, and coconut. It is also present in other tropical oils.

There are 3 macronutrients that you'll be seeing a lot of in the guide because they are vital to good nutrition. These are carbohydrates (carbs), protein, and fat.

Carbohydrates

These are often referred to as either complex or simple, and a bodybuilding diet usually contains both simple and complex carbs. The complex carbohydrates possess a chemical
structure consisting of at least three sugars. This provides energy that's preserved over time.

On the other hand, simple carbohydrates have a chemical structure comprising no more than one or two sugars; thus, they provide fast but short-lived energy. The bodybuilding diet mainly contains complex carbohydrates that you consume throughout the day. The
simple carbohydrates are eaten right after training to speed up muscle recovery. Complex carbs are contained in whole grain bread, beans, grains, pasta, and most vegetables. However, simple carbohydrates are found in fruits and sugary foods like juices, sweets, and sports drinks.

Another two ways of classifying carbohydrates in bodybuilding diets are through the following;

Glycemic index (GI) - GI measures the quality of carbohydrates in food as opposed to measuring the number of carbs in the diet. By quality we mean, how quickly a person's blood sugar levels rise after eating. According to this classification, the higher the GI, the faster the blood sugar will increase after the food has been eaten. High GI begins from 70, while a medium GI ranges from 56 - 69, and then a low GI ranges from 55 to lesser.

The GI is not a straightforward formula for lowering blood sugar. Several factors may affect this type of classification, including how the food is prepared (for example, cooked, fried, fried, or fried) and what other foods are consumed with it. Foods that break down and are absorbed by the body typically have a high GI.

Glycemic load (GL) - In 1997, a nutritionist and epidemiologist named Walter Willet from the Harvard Public Health School designed a more resourceful way to assess carbohydrate load compared to the GI. The Glycemic load factors the amount of food eaten, while the glycemic index does not. The glycemic load of a particular diet is determined by multiplying the amount of net carb in a meal portion by the glycemic index; then, you divide this number by 100.

To get the net carbohydrates, you take the total amount of carbs and subtract its dietary fiber content. For instance, the glycemic index of popcorn is 72, which is considered high, but two cup doses contain 10 net carbohydrates with a glycemic load of 7, which is deemed to be below.

PROTEIN

Your muscle is fundamentally made up of water and protein. The protein increases a person's muscle mass, but not all of the protein consumed in meals gets directed to the muscle. Adequate protein intake helps preserve the muscle tissue as well as enhance recovery from all the strenuous weight-bearing workouts that are done. This is because weight-bearing exercises significantly damage the human muscle tissue. Hence, subsequent muscle growth and repair demands a minimum recovery period of 24 hours. If it happens that there is too little protein consumed, the bodybuilder's muscle mass will suffer, leading to a decline in metabolism. Most bodybuilding diets recommend 1 to 1.5 grams of protein on a daily basis for every pound of lean body weight (your weight without the fats and obesity).

A day-to-day consumption of more than 3g per kilogram can lead to serious health problems and often kidney damage. Protein found in lean meats, tofu, eggs, poultry & fish, and soy products can cause this.

FATS

Fat is a pertinent macronutrient in a bodybuilder's diet in order to maintain a healthy metabolism. There are 4 types of fats, namely, trans, saturated, monosaturated, and polyunsaturated fat. The amount of saturated and trans fats is limited based on the amount of fat consumed. Heavy consumption is a risk factor for obesity, heart disease, diabetes, high cholesterol, and specific cancer. Foods comprising high doses of trans and saturated fats include whole milk products, butter, pastries, coconut, fried foods, palm, and other tropical oils. All meats with visible fat also contain saturated fat. Polyunsaturated and Monounsaturated fats are good fats because they reduce the chances of ailments such as diabetes, heart disease, obesity, and high cholesterol. These fats are contained in foods like flax & olive, fish, avocados, peanut, canola, corn, safflower, soybean, sunflower, and cottonseed oils.

Besides these macronutrients, the other two crucial factors in a bodybuilding diet to consider are water and the rate of meal consumption. It is recommended that a bodybuilder drinks water, a minimum of 8 to 8 ounces every day. Also, bodybuilders take about a quarter cup of water every 15 minutes during their workout. This is key because water helps control appetite, and drinking cold water speeds up your metabolism.

Also, the content and quantity of meals are essential, just as the quality and timing. This is especially true right before and right after a workout. One effective way to burn fat is to increase your body's metabolism. The process of digesting meals burns calories by itself, so the idea of the diet is to eat more often to make the process more efficient. Most bodybuilding diets recommend 6 to 8 smaller meals a day, starting with breakfast. Carbs are essential right after exercise because the body's glycogen stores (a compound that's easily converted to glucose energy) get depleted. Many bodybuilding nutritionists recommend that a post-workout meal contains twice as many proteins, calories, and carbs as other meals during the day. Pre-workout meals should be high in carbohydrates because this will help improve exercise performance and promote muscle recovery.

Now, it's easy to get lost in your desire for muscles and fitness, but it's also essential to take precautions. Under the supervision of an expert on healthcare, a bodybuilding diet can be a healthy way to increase weight and strength. However, caution should be exercised with food supplements, especially protein powders. This is because excessive protein intake has proven to lead to serious health problems like dehydration and kidney damage.

Bodybuilders need to discuss supplements with their doctors. Steroids like the human growth hormone and testosterone are other substances to be wary of. These should only
be used for medical reasons and prescribed by a credible doctor. This reason is that exercise is a significant component of the diet. People who have arthritis or any joint problems should discuss the exercise program with their doctor before engaging in any activities. Making substantial changes to a person's diet should be done in small steps to allow the body to adapt to the changes. Any sudden rise or reduction in calories can cause the body to store or accumulate fat.

Research and General Acceptance

Dieting for bodybuilders is generally accepted by the medical and bodybuilding communities. It is considered an effective and safe way to reduce fat and increase muscle mass in the body. However, the exact ratio of proteins, fats, and carbohydrates is not generally accepted.

For instance, although protein is considered an essential nutrient in weight loss for repairing broken-down muscles and their growth and maintenance, the recommended daily protein consumption is about 0.8 g/kg. Studies, however, show that more protein is needed for weight lifting. The number of proteins required by a bodybuilder is higher than that of a regular person, however, it shouldn't be more than 1.5-2 g/kg. However, even these figures are based on the person's activity level. Research by scientists in the field has revealed that muscles double the rate of protein synthesis after training and remain elevated for a minimum of 24 hours.

Hence, the number of carbohydrates inside a bodybuilder's diet can range from 40 to 60%, but still, they may not be as effective as expected. Inadequate carb consumption can have a negative effect on exercise duration and performance. Several other research has shown that the dominant factor in weight loss is reduced caloric consumption. However, people are devising their schemes and methods, but since the 1980s, researchers have done much research on bodybuilding nutrition, and it would be unwise to disregard them.

How many calories are enough calories?

This is a big question, and we'll do our best to provide an answer that works for as many people as possible. The easiest part is understanding that you need to eat more calories than your body burns. The hardest part is figuring out exactly how many calories your meal contains. Unfortunately, it is not a cut-and-dry answer because, once again, everybody is unique. Therefore it's difficult to standardize the exact number of calories needed during workouts. Daily caloric consumption is dependent on multiple factors such as body weight, sex, age, genetics, activity level, and so on.

Eating minimal calories while you're in your bulking training is one of the biggest mistakes you can make. The bulk adds weight as well as mass to increase overall strength. Thus as a general rule, a bodybuilder should consume a minimum of 2,500
calories per week. This should result in about a pound of added mass per week. The extra calories consumed are essential to achieving the results you want.

The most crucial part of bulking is making sure you eat more calories. However, another essential thing to do is know what these calories comprise. What exactly should your 'high-calorie diet look like in order for you to gain weight?"

So far, we've discussed calorie goals and the macros that your body needs. Now is the time to discuss what foods you should eat to achieve your bulk goals.

As you may already know, there are healthy and unhealthy ways to approach bulking. It makes a big difference whether you eat nutritious homemade meals or eat junk food all day to get your macro. The best and healthiest option for you is to eat right, which means you have to prepare your meals yourself. The following food options support fit pure bulk.

Key protein foods

- Chicken breast is one very good source of lean protein as it provides about 26 grams of protein for every 3 ounces.

- Seafood is a good source of protein because they are usually low in fat. Fishes such as salmon contain a little more fat but provide healthy omega-3 fatty acids.

- Milk, yogurt, and cheese are dairy products that are excellent protein sources. They also contain vitamin D and calcium. Greek yogurt and cottage cheese are good protein-rich snacks. They can be eaten alone, mixed with berries, or in a smoothie to add protein.

- Lean Beef has more fat compared to white poultry such as chicken. It is advisable to choose low-fat cuts of meat. Lean beef also presents an excellent vitamin B12, iron, and zinc source.

- Beans can serve as an incredible alternative to animal protein. Unlike animal protein, beans offer a beneficial dietary fiber.

Also, adding protein powder can be an easy way to get more protein into your system, and 2 very healthy alternatives are casein protein and whey protein.

- Casein Protein - is also a complete protein that provides all nine essential amino acids. This slowly digestible protein releases amino acids slowly. Your body may benefit from consuming casein at bedtime to promote recovery and reduce muscle breakdown while sleeping.

Whey Protein - is a complete source of protein. This means that it has all nine essential amino acids. It contains relatively little lactose, so it may be ideal for those who are hypersensitive to lactose. The addition of whey protein combined with resistance training has been shown to improve muscle synthesis and promote muscle tissue growth.

Key carbohydrates foods
- Old-fashioned oats - are a great way to get carbs and more calories in your food. They are delightful in the morning for breakfast mixed with Greek yogurt for protein or a post-workout smoothie in the afternoon.

- Sweet Potatoes - These are a great source of carbs filled with nutrients. They are just right for a post-workout meal that helps to restore glycogen levels.

- Fruits are of all sizes and shapes and can provide variety to your customers 'diet. Fruits also provide essential nutrients and antioxidants. These provide reasonable protection against cell damage. Bananas are a great snack after a workout because they provide carbohydrates and potassium to help with recovery. You should eat fresh fruit instead of dried fruit. Dried fruits are usually full of added sugars—the natural sugars in the fruit better support your customers 'bulk goals.

- Rice - White rice has arguably been considered one of the best meat-enhancing foods. It provides a large number of carbohydrates per serving and is an easy filler. Combine rice with some vegetables and protein for a perfect post-workout meal.

- Whole Grain Bread - Bread has gotten a bad rap lately, mainly due to the recent explosion of low-carb diets. But if your customers 'goal is to grow and increase muscle mass, the last thing they want is a low-carb diet.

Bread is a great way to get carbs quickly and easily, and you can easily add a little peanut butter and sliced banana to add carbs.

- Vegetables – these are an excellent source of complex carbohydrates. They do not provide large amounts of carbohydrates compared to other food options, but they are essential for maintaining overall health during your customers 'filling. Vegetables are full of essential vitamins and nutrients. The vitamins and minerals in vegetables help support growth and repair. Ask your customers to mix many steamed vegetables with rice and potatoes to get the vitamins they need.

Key Healthy fats

- Eggs -These are a great source of healthy fats. In addition, they also act as healthy sources of protein. They are a great breakfast option, along with oatmeal and fresh fruit.

- Nuts - Foods rich in energy and nutrients; nuts contain healthy monounsaturated fats. Nuts and peanut butter are full of essential trace elements and minerals such as magnesium, zinc, selenium, and phosphorus. These micronutrients and minerals are critical for maintaining a healthy nutritional state to support muscle mass building.

- Avocados - A reliable source of monounsaturated fatty acids. These fatty acids help reduce inflammation. In addition, avocados are rich in antioxidants and vitamin E, which support cardiovascular health.
- Coconut & Olive Oil is an excellent way to add healthy fats to your diet. Encourage your customers to make small changes, such as using them in cooking or preparing meals. Making these changes is good for adding healthy fats and more calories to your diet without leaving your customers too full.

From time to time, it's good to sit down and analyze your overall dining plan so as to determine your caloric needs and plan your macronutrient consumption. So once you are all set, you can begin planning your snack and meal ideas. Decide the best time for you to prepare and eat meals as you start your bulking journey. Combining a nutrient rich diet with the right kind of exercise should get you to your bulking or cutting goals.

Remember, as a bodybuilder; it's more than just increasing muscle size, improving appearance, and developing overall strength. It's about being the best you possible.

Nonetheless, to build the muscles you want, you need to focus on challenging resistance training to achieve bigger muscles. The following are 3 possible mechanisms of muscle hypertrophy:

- Metabolic stress

- Mechanical stress

- Muscle damage

Nutrition for Bodybuilding

As stated earlier, for you to reduce body fat or increase your muscle mass, you have to concentrate on consuming the right amount of calories. It's also pertinent to concentrate on your consumption of macronutrients and your eating strategy.

The bodybuilding community is still undecided on the number of meals a bodybuilder should eat per day. Specific reviews suggest that a person can consume about three to six meals every day. It states that the timing of meals and exercises does not affect fat reduction or muscle maintenance.

A bodybuilder can choose from several different foods to prepare their meal plan during the week. In general, you should focus on foods that provide adequate calories and nutrients. During the cutting phase, it is desirable for the bodybuilder to feel fuller with a certain amount of calories. However, it is possible to struggle with the opposite issue during the bulk phase. This is because you may need to continue eating to reach the high-calorie intake goals despite feeling full.

You should also note that many foods contain more than one macronutrient. Nuts, for instance, can provide both protein and fat. The specific needs of a person for each food vary according to size and daily caloric needs.

A 7 Day Meal Program

As you must know, meal plans differ from one person to another based on size, gender, goals, and size. In addition, different nutritionists and coaches can make other recommendations depending on whether a person following a bodybuilding meal plan is trying to build lean muscle mass or cut excess fat.

According to a study published in the JISSN (Journal of the International Society of Sports Nutrition), bodybuilders consume more calories than most athletes preparing for a competition.

The most abundant macro-nutrition in the bodybuilder's diet at all stages was carbohydrates from whole grains, fruits, and vegetables. According to the same study, the protein derived from nuts, dairy products, white meat, and seafood was the second most abundant macronutrient in the bodybuilder's diet.

The study found that bodybuilders ate fewer eggs and red meat, even though they still got protein from these sources. However, note that doses vary from person to person. You should calculate your own macro needs for dose recommendations or consult a certified nutritionist. The following is a proper seven-day meal plan for bodybuilding.

- Day 1

Breakfast - Scrambled eggs, oatmeal, and fried vegetables

Snack - Whey protein shake

Lunch - Grilled chicken breast, fried sweet potatoes, and

vegetables Snack – Carrot sticks and hard-boiled egg

Dinner - Fried fish, brown rice, and green beans

- Day 2

Breakfast – Fresh berries with protein pancakes

Snack – Almonds and apple slices

Lunch - Low-fat minced burger placed on salad, onions, green beans, and

tomatoes Snack - protein shake

Dinner – Paprika fried with prawns and brown rice with spinach

- Day 3

Breakfast – Almonds & Greek yogurt, or walnuts, fresh berries, and whole

grains Snack - Protein shake

Lunch – Broccoli with spinach salad and grilled fish

Snack – Mushrooms, peppers with egg white omelet

Dinner - Chicken breast placed on top of sweet potatoes, fresh salsa, and side dishes

- Day 4

Breakfast – Oatmeal with egg white and berries

Snack - Turkey breast with celery and carrots

Lunch - Beef steak with mushrooms and broccoli

Snack – Natural peanut butter with apples

Dinner – Mixed green salad, brown rice, and fried fish

- Day 5

Breakfast - Protein shake and oatmeal

Snack - Hard-boiled egg whites with cucumber and sliced

peppers Lunch - Grilled chicken together with tomato salad
and white beans Snack – Nuts and berries with Greek yogurt

Dinner - Grilled fish with green beans and quinoa

- Day 6

Breakfast – Cheese with egg whites, herbs, peppers, and Ezekiel
bread Snack - Protein shake

Lunch - Grilled chicken breast with black beans, paprika, and onion
placed on romaine lettuce

Snack – Almond and apple

Dinner - Tenderloin with asparagus and sweet potatoes

- Day 7

Breakfast - Greek yogurt with berries and whole grains

Snack - Turkey breast with celery sticks and carrots

Lunch - Grilled chicken breast on spinach with almonds and sliced
strawberries Snack - Protein shake

Dinner - Prawns fried over brown rice with paprika, broccoli, and onion

As a bodybuilder, you should also acknowledge the use of nutritional
supplements. These can play an essential role in providing nutrients to you as
you train. Pursuant to a new review, some vitamins, and supplements that can
help a bodybuilder are as follows:

- Creatine monohydrate (take 3g per day)
- Beta-alanine (take 3-5g daily)

- Citrulline malate (take 8 g per day)

- Caffeine (take 5-6 milligrams per kilogram of body weight

daily) • Omega-3 supplements

However, when choosing a supplement, you should be aware that the Food and
Drug Administration's (FDA) supplement regulation is not as strict as medicines.
Thus people should seek the advice of their doctor or nutritionist when choosing
a dietary supplement or milkshake.

Now, as you must know, bodybuilders, diet gurus and trainers, who are worth their salt will tell you that more than 50% of their bodybuilding endeavor is dieting. This is very reasonable, especially when it comes to a beginner. After layoffs, beginners or those who return to the gym can expect to receive severe strength and weight gain from a regular exercise program, but not without a solid nutrition program.

The bottom line is that the more serious you are in your diet, the more serious your winnings will be. If you combed the literature on weightlifting, you would quickly learn that relatively little research has been done on exercise techniques that grow strength and muscle mass. However, there have been numerous studies on the effects of supplements and diets. The studies reveal that paying attention to the macronutrients, meal timing, calories, and certain supplements will significantly impact a bodybuilder's results.

10 Basic Nutritional Rules

To further help you out with this, we've outlined 10 essential nutrition and additional rules that everyone can learn and follow indefinitely. If you follow these rules and also follow your lifting program, your body will thank you for it.

1. Focus on protein

Take a minimum of 1 gram of protein per kilogram of body weight on a daily basis. Protein provides amino acids that are used as the building blocks of muscle protein. Although the recommended daily dose of protein is set at less than half a gram per kilogram of body weight for a typical person, research also has it that athletes, especially those interested in muscle strength and mass, need about twice the amount.

Beginners should actually try to get about 1.5 grams of protein per pound of bodyweight daily. This should be done for the first six months of training. This is because then your muscles will respond faster to exercise then. For a 180-pound person, this means an initial 270 grams a day and then 180 grams a day afterward.

Your protein selection should be based primarily on low-fat animal proteins such as chicken, beef, eggs, turkey, fish, and dairy products. These are the complete protein sources, which means that they provide the body with all the critical amino acids that are defined as those that the body cannot produce on its own.

2. Carbohydrate up

Consume from 2 to 3 grams of carbs for every pound of bodyweight daily. As you know, right behind carbohydrates is protein in importance for muscle growth.

The carbs are maintained in the muscles as glycogen which keeps your muscles complete and extensive and also nourishes them during exercise. A beginner weighing 180 pounds needs 360 to 540 grams of carbs every day to gain weight.

Most meals should use slow-digesting carbohydrate sources like oatmeal, whole grains, beans, sweet potatoes, vegetables, and fruits.

3. Do not Avoid grease

Around 20-30% of your daily calories should come from fat like a bodybuilder. As opposed to the sedentary population who are advised to eliminate saturated fat consumption, 5-10% of your fat calories should be saturated. This is because diets that are higher in fat - especially those with more saturated and monounsaturated fats - seem to maintain testosterone levels better than low-fat foods. Also, remember that it is vital to maintain optimal testosterone levels in building strength and muscle mass. This is also vital to avoid fat growth.

Thus, choose red meat from saturated fats, like minced meat and steak, since they also provide high-quality protein. Other foods include nut mixtures, avocados, peanut butter, and olive oil.

4. Number of calories

You need to stay in a positive calorie balance by taking in more calories than you consume to get quality mass. Burning more calories than you consume is a negative balance and your body may go into a state of the economy and will not support new muscle growth.

Therefore, a 180-pound person should get about 3,600 calories a day. With Rules 1, 2, and 3 in mind, 20-30% of these calories should be from protein, 40-60% from carbohydrates, and 20-30% from fat.

5. Eat often

Needless to say, you must eat a high-protein, high-carbohydrate meal every 2-3 hours. This will help to maintain a consistent amino acids supply and energy for growth. This
will help you gain weight and stay lean. The idea is to keep each meal about the same size. If you eat a 1,200-calorie lunch, you're probably not eating 2-3 hours later. Aim for at least 6 meals a day and shoot at 8, which for a 180-pound man would mean 500 to 600 calories per meal.

6. Shake it

Before and after your workout, you will get at least 20 grams of protein in a convenient milkshake form. Protein shakes are considered a dietary supplement, but we consider them a substantial meal to be enjoyed at critical times of the day. While your diet should consist primarily of unprocessed whole foods, sometimes a protein shake is a much better option. An example is 30 minutes just before a workout. To prepare your muscle for your next activity and get ahead in the muscle recovery process, drink a milkshake with 20 grams of whey protein or a mixture of whey and casein and about 40 grams slower, melting of carbohydrates.

Immediately after exercises in the 60-minute window, take another 20-40 grams of liquid protein and 60-100 grams of easily-digestible carbs.

7. Time your consumption of carbs and eat the right ones

Consume slow carbs 30 minutes before you begin workouts. Also, make these fast carbs after your workout and choose a slower burning carbohydrate for most meals, even before training. Research has shown that when athletes eat slower digestible carbohydrates, not only do they have more energy and less fatigue during training, but they burn more fat during training. Also, they experience less hunger throughout the day. Good low-carbohydrate options include oatmeal, fruit, and wholemeal bread.

However, after working out, choose fast-digesting carbohydrates such as plain bagel, white bread, baked potato, or maybe even a sports drink. The idea is to raise the level of the anabolic hormone insulin, which drives the carbs you eat into the muscle cells, where they are stored as glycogen.

Insulin also helps amino acids get into muscle cells for growth. It is critical in generating creatine required by the muscles and increases muscle protein synthesis, one of the significant processes muscle fibers grow. Typically, you want to keep your insulin levels under control for several health reasons, but immediately after a hard workout, an insulin spike is desirable.

8. Eat before bed

Enjoy 30 to 40 grams of micellar casein protein shake or 1 cup of low-fat cottage cheese with 2-3 tablespoons of flaxseed oil. You can also have it with 2 ounces of nuts or 2-3 peanut butter tablespoons before bed at night. Know that you mainly fast for about 7-9 hours when you sleep. Whenever food is not available, your body then searches for amino acids in your muscle fibers with which the brain can feed. This isn't a good thing
for a person who wants to grow and lose weight. Thus, the answer is not less sleep; the solution is eating the right food just before you go to bed.
Slow-digesting proteins and healthy fats are the best options you have. This is because these foods help slow down
digestion, providing a steady amount of fuel amino acids and minimizing the body's tendency to use muscle. Casein, a major protein contained in milk is

one proper alternative you can try.

9. Use creatine

You should have 3-5 grams of creatine before and after your workout shakes because creatine is one very effective supplement. Many researchers, nutritionists, and doctors have agreed that creatine works well for most athletes, regardless of age or sex. After multiple studies on the supplement, the consensus is that it is effective and safe. Taking creatine as a monohydrate or any other form can help you gain up to 10 pounds of lean muscle. Also, it can increase your strength at the gym by 10% and produce a significantly higher pump during exercise with no side effects whatsoever.

10. Use HMB (hydroxy-beta-methyl butyrate)

It is advisable to take 1-3 grams of HMB with food when you wake up in the morning, before and after exercise. This is also good at bedtime during the first 3 months of practice. In addition to creatine, suitable for bodybuilders of all levels, another great supplement for beginners is HMB, a branched-chain amino acid leucine metabolite. This substance prevents muscle breakdown and stimulates muscle growth which is especially helpful for novice trainees. When you reach the 3-month limit, you can switch to 5-10 grams of leucine simultaneously.

26 Foods that can help you Build Muscle Mass

The importance of nutrition in your quest to gain lean muscle cannot be overemphasized. To begin, it's essential to tax your body with the appropriate physical activities. However, without the help of proper nutritional support, you'll progress smoothly.

As you know, protein-rich foods are very crucial to muscle growth, just as carbohydrates and fats are for the energy they supply. If the aim is to gain lean muscle, you should exercise regularly and eat more calories each day from meat-building foods. The following are 26 foods to help you build muscle mass.

1. Eggs - Eggs contain high-quality protein, healthy fats, and other vital nutrients like choline and B vitamins. Proteins comprise amino acids, and eggs contain large amounts of the amino acid leucine, which is key to muscle growth.

B vitamins are also essential for many processes in your body, including energy production.
2. Salmon - Salmon is an excellent choice for muscle building and overall health. Each serving of 3 ounces contains around 17 grams of protein, several essential B vitamins, and nearly 2 grams of omega-3 fatty acids. Omega-3 fatty acids are

essential to muscle health and can even increase muscle growth during exercise programs.

3. Chicken breast - There is a good reason why chicken breast is considered a staple of muscle building. They are full of protein, and each 3-ounce serving contains around 26 grams of high-quality protein. They are also rich in niacin, B vitamins, and B6, which can be especially important if you are active.

Now, these vitamins help the body of a bodybuilder function properly during physical activity or workout, which is essential for achieving optimal muscle growth. Also, some tests have shown that a more protein-rich diet that includes chicken can promote fat loss.

4. Greek yogurt - This dairy contains high-quality protein and a mixture of fast-digesting whey protein and slow-digesting casein protein. Some studies have shown that people's low-fat mass increases when they consume fast- and slow-digesting milk proteins. But then, not every dairy product is made equal.

For instance, Greek yogurt often contains around twice as much protein as the regular yogurts you know. Besides the fact that Greek yogurt is a good snack at any time, eating it after training or before bedtime can be helpful because it contains fast and slow digesting proteins.

5. Tuna – Besides the fact that this contains 20 grams of protein, an 85-gram serving of tuna offers your high body amounts of vitamin A and multiple B vitamins. This includes niacin, B12, and B6. These nutrients are essential for optimal energy, health, and exercise performance.

Also, tuna contains large amounts of omega-3 fatty acids, supporting muscle health. This can be very helpful to older adults. Studies have shown that omega-3 fatty acids can slow the loss of muscle mass and strength with age.

6. Lean beef -Beef is full of high-quality protein, minerals, creatine, and B vitamins. Specific research has even shown that eating lean red meat can increase the amount of lean mass achieved through weight training.

However, even if you are working towards the formation of muscles, it may be best to choose beef that supports muscle growth without providing too many extra calories. For instance, 3 ounces of 70% lean minced beef has 228 calories and an incredible 15 grams of fat.

Nonetheless, the same number of 95% lean minced beef contains slightly more protein and only 145 in calories and 5 grams of fat.

7. Shrimp -These are almost pure protein, and each 3-ounce serving possesses 1 gram of fat, no carbs, and 18 grams of protein. Although healthy fats and carbs are essential in your overall diet, including shrimps in it is a simple method for getting muscle-building protein without too many unnecessary calories. Similar to many other animal proteins, shrimp comprise a large amount of the amino acid leucine, which you know is critical to optimal muscle growth.

8. Soybeans -Half a cup of cooked soybeans can provide your body with 14 grams of protein, multiple vitamins, minerals, and healthy unsaturated fats. Soybeans are a prosperous source of iron, vitamin K, and phosphorus. Iron is used to transport and store oxygen in your muscles and blood. Also, a deficiency in it can impair these functions.

This is particularly the case for young women who are at risk of developing iron deficiency due to menstrual blood loss.

9. Cottage cheese - A cup of low-fat cottage cheese provides your body with 28 grams of protein. This includes a high dose of the essential muscle-building amino acid leucine.

Like the other dairy products, this food can be purchased with differing fat contents. The fatty versions include the creamy cottage cheese, which contains more calories.

Choosing the best type of cottage cheese will depend on the number of extra calories you want to add to your diet. No matter what type you choose, it's an excellent muscle building snack.

10. Turkey breast -A 3-ounce dose of turkey breast comprises about 25 grams of protein and almost no fat or carbs. Turkey breast is also a good source of vitamin B niacin as it helps process carbs and fats in your body.

Optimal vitamin B levels can also help with muscle-building over time by supporting your body's ability to exercise.

11. Tilapia -Although tilapia does not have lots of omega-3 fatty acids when compared to salmon, it is still protein-packed seafood. A dose of 3 ounces offers around 21 grams of protein as well as reasonable amounts of selenium and vitamin B12.

Vitamin B12 is key to the formation of healthy nerves and blood cells, thereby allowing you to perform the exercise you need to grow those muscles.

12. Beans - Many different bean varieties can be part of a diet to grow lean muscle. The standard types, like surface, black, and kidney beans, possess about 15 grams of protein in a cup of about 172 grams of cooked beans.

Also, beans are an excellent source of B vitamins and fiber, as well as being rich in magnesium, iron, and phosphorus. These are the reasons that make beans a good source of plant-based protein to include in your diet. Also, remember that they can play a role in long-term health and disease prevention.

13. Protein powders - Although any good diet should concentrate on whole foods, there are times when supplements can play a vital role. If you're dealing with trouble getting enough protein from food, you may want to consider adding protein shakes to your day to-day routine. Milk protein powders like casein and whey are some of the most popular

options.

14. Edamame – This term refers to unripe soybeans. These developing beans can be discovered in pieces and are served in various foods. A cup equal to 155 grams of frozen edamame offers your body about 17 grams of protein and 8 grams of fiber. Also, it comprises large amounts of vitamin K, folate, and manganese.

Among other benefits, the folate it contains can help your body process amino acids. In fact, folate is possibly crucial to optimal muscle strength and mass, especially for the elderly.

15. Quinoa - Although high-protein foods are crucial to building lean muscle, it's also essential that you have the fuel. Carbohydrate-rich foods like this can help provide this fuel. Cooked Quinoa possesses about 40 grams of carbs, 5 grams of fiber, 8 grams of protein, and copious amounts of phosphorus and magnesium.

Magnesium aids the proper functioning of your nerves and muscles. These two are used every time you exercise.

16. Scallops – Like tilapia, shrimp, and low-fat poultry, scallops offer very little protein. To add protein to your diet without taking too many calories, these very low-fat sources are very reasonable.3 ounces of scallops can provide about 20 grams of protein and less than 100 calories.

17. Lean Jerky - Sometimes, you may want high-quality protein from your meat on the go. Thus if this is the case, lean jerky meat may be a viable option. Many different types of meat can be made into jerky, so nutritional information varies.

However, most of the fat it contains gets removed during processing. That way, almost all of the calories left in it are directly from the protein. These sources of animal protein are of high quality and stimulate muscle growth.

18. Chickpeas are also known as garbanzo beans and are a good source of protein and carbohydrates. Each cup of canned chickpeas comprises about 12 grams of protein plus 50 grams of carbs and another 10 grams of fiber.

Like many plants, chickpea protein is deemed inferior to that of animal sources. Nonetheless, it can be part of a balanced muscle-building diet.

19. Peanuts contain a mixture of fat, protein, and carbohydrates. A serving of half a cup of these offers your body 17 grams of protein, 16 grams of carbs, and vast amounts of unsaturated fats. They also hold lots of the amino acid leucine than many other plant products.

Every half cup of peanuts, representing 73 grams, contains about 425 calories. So if you're having trouble getting the much-needed calories to grow your muscle mass, consuming peanuts can be a great way to get more nutrients and calories.

Also, nuts are regarded as key to the overall healthy diet of a bodybuilder.

20. Buckwheat - This is a seed that can be ground into flour and then used to

replace traditional flour. Half a cup of these contains about 8 grams of protein. Also, it is high in fiber and other carbs. Buckwheat has become a prevalent health food due to its impressive mineral and vitamin content.

It contains lots of magnesium, B vitamins, phosphorus, and manganese. These vitamins and minerals may assist your body stay healthy and being able to carry out muscle building exercises.

21. Tofu – This is made from soy milk and is frequently used as a substitute for meat, and each half-cup of it contains 6 grams of fat, 10 grams of protein, and 2 grams of carbohydrates. Tofu is a great calcium-giving food and is essential for proper skeletal health and muscle function.

Soy protein, which is present in foods like soybeans and tofu, is considered one of the highest quality plant proteins. For all of these reasons, foods that contain soy protein are great alternatives for vegans.

22. Pork tenderloin - Pork is generally consumed in many countries. It is a thin piece of meat containing 18 grams of protein and just 2 grams of fat for every 3 ounces. Some studies have shown that pork has effects similar to other muscle-building foods such as chicken and beef.

23. Milk - This provides a combination of carbs, proteins, and fats, and similar to other dairy products, milk possesses both fast and slow-digesting proteins. This is believed to benefit muscle growth. For a fact, multiple reports have shown that people can increase their muscle mass when they drink milk, along with weight training.

24. Almonds - Half a cup of whipped almonds weighs 172 grams and provides 16 grams of protein along with lots of magnesium, vitamin E, and phosphorus. Among other functions, phosphorus can help a bodybuilder use carbohydrates and fats for energy at rest and during exercise.

Just like peanuts, almonds may be taken in moderation. This is because of its high caloric content. Half a cup of whipped almonds contains more than 400 calories.

25. Biisoni – This food, like beef, provides about 22 grams of protein per 85 grams of serving. However, some studies have shown that bison can be better than beef in terms of the risk of heart disease.

If you like consuming red meat as part of the muscle-building diet, but you are also worried about your heart's health, you can consider the replacement of beef with bison.

26. Brown rice - Although cooked brown rice contains just 5 grams of protein for each cup, it has all the carbohydrates your body needs to promote physical activity. This empowers you to exercise harder and gives your body more stimuli for your muscles to grow.

Also, certain studies have shown that rice protein supplements can produce as much muscle growth as whey protein during a weight training regimen.

Why do you need to Prep your Meals?

Individuals need to understand that preparing meals is one viable way to save time in the kitchen and money. However, most importantly, it helps you stay on track with your body formation. There's also some relief to gain from the endless hours spent dicing, slicing, and baking during an already exhausting work week. After all, once the breakfast, lunch, and/or dinner portions are made, you'll have more time with your family when you need it most.

However, preparing meals is more than just one ingenious way to organize before peak times. As stated by Amy Shapiro, who is an expert on the topic, it's also a straightforward way to help yourself eat healthier, more nutritious, and satisfying meals. How? Firstly, preparing a meal requires that you do the task at home, which automatically takes you ahead in the healthy eating department. Also, planning your meals in advance will help you prepare for success throughout the week. The following are some reasons why training your meals helps you further along.

1. Regular dining intervals

You've probably heard that you shouldn't go to the grocery store hungry. Apply this theory to your crumbling belly on a busy workday. Also, include it in those inevitable moments between appointments when you dig into your dangerously handy trash can. I mean those moments when you don't know what to eat, or you allow yourself to be too hungry and tend to eat foods you haven't planned for. Preparing a meal ensures you have healthy food ready, and you can avoid making bad decisions due to excessive hunger or overeating. Now that we all work from home and have access to refrigerators and snacks round the clock, healthy pre-prepared meals are more important than ever before.

2. Water retention and decreased swelling

When you prepare your food, you know exactly what it entails. So assuming, you're sensitive to sodium or tend to feel swollen after the night, you can modify your own recipe to eliminate these symptoms. When you eat out or order the meals, restaurants have one goal: to make sure the food tastes good. This often means too much salt and fat in your deliveries. By preparing your food yourself, you can avoid latent or excess sodium and saturated fat, which all means that you'll feel good the next day.

3. You control what goes into your body when you prepare your meal.

Meal planning has to do with dictating the quality and source of your meals. This includes the category of meat you want, its freshness, and how many packaged or processed ingredients you intend to use. For instance, making your own salad dressing takes less than 5 minutes and helps avoid excessive chemicals that come into the pre bottled item. This also holds true for frozen meals, sandwiches, granola bars, and other ready meals. By preparing a meal, you can ensure you eat what you want. I guarantee
you will also feel better and if you're trying to switch to a more herbal diet, preparing meals is a great way to get into it.

4. You can limit the added sugar

The idea is simple: your food and preparation; hence, nothing goes in without your knowledge. The general idea is that healthy foods rarely contain too much sugar. Preparing your food helps avoid the extra sugar and, in turn, the side effects that come with such. For instance, by making yogurt parfait yourself instead of buying one from Starbucks or deli, you can save over 8 teaspoons of sugar.

5. You control the dosage, and besides, it's an excellent excuse to eat extra vegetables.

The thing is, when you prepare your own meal, you get to decide how many servings you get from one recipe. The chain restaurants want to entice you with portion sizes and want you to feel like you're getting value for your money. When preparing meals, you know exactly how many ounces of carbs, protein, and vegetables you get. You can always make a plate for your total well-being - add an extra serving of black beans, roasted carrots, boiled quinoa, or tofu to the cereal bowl if that's what you want.

Generally, preparing meals can help you implement healthy eating habits despite your everyday hectic and busy schedule with precise calorie and dose management. Cooking also helps lessen food waste. Thus you can help the environment while maintaining a perfect work-life balance.

Top 20 Meal Recipes to Build Muscle

Male chefs work in high-end restaurants as well as kick-ass TV programs. It is now widely accepted that men love healthy, good, and even better, prepared at home food.

These inspiring recipes combine delicious ingredients along with creative cooking techniques that will satisfy every man who loves decent food. Also, they're packed with all sorts of healthy ingredients to help build muscle and keep you lean, fresh, and ripped.

Recipe 1: Cedar Plank Trout along with Asian Guacamolella

Here you can add a delicious trout flavor to your protein-filled meal when you cook on top of the cedar. The best part is, cedar does not come with extra calories!

Serving - 4
Preparation time from beginning to end -45 minutes

Preparation - 20 minutes and cooking - 25 minutes

Below are the ingredients:

- 2 cedar planks (soaked in water for a minimum of 2 hours)

- 1 lb wild trout fillets (cut into 4 pieces)

- 1-2 spoons of roasted sesame oil

- Sea salt & freshly crushed black pepper

- Asian Guacamole

- 1 avocado peeled & stoned

- 1 tbsp grated fresh ginger

- 2 chopped onions

- Fresh mint leaves (1 cup)

- Fresh coriander leaves & stems (1 cup)

- Jalapeno, stem & seeds (1 cup)

- 1 lime juice

- Sea salt (¼ teaspoon)

How to prepare:

Firstly, place half of the grill on medium heat. Secondly, drain the cedar boards, place the trout fillets on the skin side down, and add sesame oil before seasoning it with salt and pepper. Put on the grill on the opposite side of the heater. Afterward, cover and cook for 20-25 minutes. Then remove and set aside.

Thirdly, put all the guacamole ingredients in the food processor and stir until pureed and well mixed—taste and, if necessary, season with salt or lime juice. Then, you can serve the trout with fair guacamole.

The nutritional value is 280 calories, 17 grams total fat, 25 grams of proteins, and 7 grams of Carbohydrates. It also comprises 1 gram of sugar, 4 grams of fiber, 66 milligrams of cholesterol, and 349 milligrams of sodium.

Recipe 2: Asian pork rides

This takes some effort to make, but it's all worth it. To make a whole batch of 30, freeze half by placing them in one layer on a sheet pan 1 inch apart before freezing completely. Then transfer all the iced dumplings into a resealable bag and store them frozen until use.
Doses: 30

Preparation from beginning to the end - 1 hour plus

Preparation -1 hour 20 minutes, cooking – 10 minutes

Below are the ingredients:

- Gyoza wrappers (1 pack)

- Dried and chopped shrimp (2 teaspoons)

- Sherry (2 teaspoons)

- Chopped cabbage

- Kosher salt (half teaspoon)

- Minced pork (1 pound)

- Chopped chives (1 bunch)

- Grounded garlic (1 big clove)

- Grated and peeled ginger (1 inch)

- Low-sodium soy sauce (3 tablespoons)

- Oyster sauce (1 tablespoon)

- Sugar (1 tablespoon)

- Sesame oil (half teaspoon)

- 1 big beaten egg

- Freshly ground black pepper (half teaspoon)

- Cornstarch (1 heaping tablespoon)

- Unflavoured rice wine vinegar (1/3 cups)

- Low-sodium soy sauce (1/4 cups)

- Sriracha (1 teaspoon)

- 1 diagonally sliced onion

How to prepare:

Firstly, mix all ingredients contained in the filling in a large bowl and mix thoroughly with your clean hands before setting it aside. Secondly, mix the dipping sauce ingredients in a small bowl and set aside.

First, add water to a small bowl for the dumplings and keep it close. Hold the wrap in the palm of your hand. Immerse your fingers in water, then ensure water hits the
perimeter of the wrapper. Spoon a teaspoon of the filling to the wrapper's center before you fold it in half. Fold by making a slight bulge at the edge of the top wrap, then press the crease firmly to secure it to the dumpling's bottom. Continue this process until the
lump is in half and the filling has condensed on the inside. Afterward, place the dumplings on the baking sheet and continue to assemble.

As for steaming towels, first, add an inch of water to a large saucepan and boil. Place a few cabbage leaves in a steaming basket or a bamboo vaporizer or steaming basket. Put the dumplings in the steaming basket, then keep them in the pan to prevent the dumplings from touching the water. Cover and steam until the wrapper is translucent and the filling is cooked firm. Transfer it to your saucepan and garnish with extra chives or sliced onions before serving.

Now, cook the dumplings on the stove by first adding 1-2 tablespoons of vegetable oil to the pan and heating it. Once hot, put your dumplings in the pan (pleat side up) and cook for 1-2 minutes. Then carefully add water to the pan to cover the bottom and place the lid on the pan. Bring to boil for another 2-3 minutes before transferring to a tray. You can garnish with chives or chopped scallions before serving with dipping sauce.

The nutritional value is 60 calories, 3 grams total fat, 4 grams of protein, 5 grams of carbohydrates, and 1 gram in sugar. Also, it offers 17 milligrams of cholesterol and 187 milligrams of sodium.

Recipe 3: tenderloin Breakfast slides

Do not fret; steak is healthy for breakfast. Each breakfast slider comprises 2 ounces of beef, which is a great way to enjoy beef in a dose-controlled manner for your mornings.

Serving - 3

Preparation from beginning to end - 33 minutes and the marinating time Preparation -20 minutes and cooking - 13 minutes

Below are the ingredients:

- Tenderloin for topping
- Maple whiskey (2 ounces)
- One tablespoon molasses
- two tablespoons sugar
- ¼ cups of water
- Lean sirloin (6 oz)
- Light vegan butter (2 teaspoons)
- Halved English wholemeal muffins (3)
- Non-fat cream cheese (3 tablespoons)
- Sugar-free maple syrup (3 teaspoons)
- Strawberry jelly or fruit spread (6 tablespoons)
- 3 fried eggs

How to prepare:

Firstly, mix the marinade ingredients in an airtight container, then place the beef in a container. You may allow it to marinate for 48 hours. Secondly, set the oven to bake when you are ready to assemble. Thirdly, place the cast iron skillet on the stove for heating.

After 5 minutes, remove and place 2 teaspoons of vegan butter inside a pan before putting one tip of the tenderloin on the pan.

Afterward, return to the oven and bake for 3-4 minutes per half. Remove the tenderloin tip from the pan and allow simmering on the cutting board. Repeat the previous process with the other end of the tenderloin before you cut the tenderloin into long strips.

The next thing is to assemble the sandwich and toast the English muffins before mixing the maple syrup and cream cheese in a small bowl. Then fry the eggs in the same pan you used in making your tenderloin. After that, remove the toasted English muffins and place them on your small plates.

Then whip one side with fresh maple cheese and the other with jelly before putting the egg on top of the cream cheese side. Afterward, put 2 ounces of tenderloin on the jelly side and carefully place the egg side over the steak, and there is your yummy meal!

The nutritional value per slider is 310 in calories, 4.5 grams in fat, 27 grams of proteins, and 42 grams of carbohydrates. It also provides 18 grams of sugar, 4 grams of fiber, 50 milligrams of cholesterol, and 480 milligrams of sodium.

Recipe 4: Balsamico and garlic chicken

The combination of balsamic vinegar & garlic with mushrooms give the chicken an aromatic taste that's just right.

Serving - 4

Preparation from beginning to end - 40 minutes

Preparation -15 minutes cooking - 25 minutes

Below are the ingredients:

- 4 skinless and boneless chicken breasts (thin slices)

- Sliced mushrooms (half pounds)

- 2 tablespoons of flour
- Pepper and salt

- Garlic peeled (7 cloves)

- 3 tablespoons olive oil

- Balsamic vinegar (1/4 cups)

- Low-sodium chicken broth (3/4 cup)

- 2 bay leaves

- Half thyme

- 1 tablespoon butter

How to prepare:

Start by sprinkling your salt and pepper on the chicken to taste. Then add sauce to the flour and spread the chicken in the flour mixture. Secondly, you should heat the oil in a pan over minimal heat and fry the chicken for about 3 minutes on each side.

Thirdly, add the peeled garlic to the pan, including the mushrooms. Continue frying the chicken and stir with the mushrooms for about 3 minutes. Afterward, put bay leaves, thyme, broth, and vinegar. Allow to simmer over normal heat for 10-12 minutes and stir occasionally.

Next, remove the chicken and transfer it to a serving bowl. Continue to simmer the sauce for 5 minutes. Add your butter and remove the bay leaves.

Add sauce to the chicken and serve.

The nutritional value per serving is 446 calories, 19 grams total fat, 5 grams saturated fats, 56 grams of proteins, and 9 grams of carbs. It also has 3 grams of sugar, 1 gram of fiber, 180 milligrams of cholesterol, and 370 milligrams of sodium.

Recipe 5: Kale Italian Salad

This is great for lunch or as a light dinner. The salad comprises sunflower seeds, red peppers, white beans, and kale. The combination of proteins, healthy fats, and fiber nourishes and keeps you satisfied.

Servings - 8

From beginning to the end - 8 minutes

Preparation - 8 minutes

Below are the ingredients:

- 2 cups kale mix (premixed)
- Extra virgin olive oil (2 tablespoons)
- 1 juiced lemon
- Freshly ground pepper
- Cherry tomatoes cut in half (1 cup)
- 1 dl canned cannellini beans (drained)
- Fresh mozzarella beads (4 oz)
- Drained sliced canned roasted red pepper (half cup)
- Roasted unsalted sunflower seeds (1/3 cup)

How to prepare:

First, spread the kale mixture on a serving tray. Secondly, sprinkle lemon juice and olive oil on top of the greens. Then sprinkle with crushed pepper. Spread the tomatoes, afterward, the beans, and then the mozzarella over the cooked greens. Add red peppers layered in the middle of the salad.

Sprinkle sunflower seeds over the salad. Serve immediately.

The nutritional value per serving is 164 calories, 9 grams total fat, 2 grams saturated fats, 7 grams proteins, 12 grams carbohydrates, and 1 gram sugar. It also offers 4 grams of fiber and 7 milligrams of cholesterol, and 212 milligrams of sodium.

Recipe 6: Lemon shrimp with goat cheese

When baby shrimp are combined with thyme, goat cheese, crispy celery, cream cheese, and lemon, it makes for one very impressive appetizer.

Servings - 16

From beginning to end - 20 minutes with an extra 2 hours to cool

Preparation -20 minutes

Below are the ingredients:

- 1 pound of baby shrimp, cleaned in a sieve with extra moisture, gently pushed through the wing

- Grounded red onion (2 tablespoons)

- 1 cup chopped celery

- 1 medium lemon zest

- Grounded fresh thyme (1 tablespoon)

- 2 ounces goat cheese

- 2 ounces low-fat cream cheese
- Baby arugula (2 cups)

- 1 teaspoon olive oil

- 1 pinch of salt

- 1 pinch pepper

How to prepare:

Firstly, cover a small baking dish as shown with cooking spray. Secondly, mix the remaining ingredients in a bowl and mix well apart from the arugula, olive oil, pepper, and salt. For the third step, gently press the shrimp mixture into the baking dish and use a plastic wrap to cover before refrigerating for 2 hours or overnight.

The fourth step is to season the arugula with pepper, salt, and olive oil. Then, dip the arugula on a serving plate. After that, you can turn the shrimp mixture from the bowl over the arugula.

The nutrition value for every serving is 123 calories, 8 grams of total fat: 8, 2 grams saturated fats, 8 grams proteins, 4 grams carbohydrates, 2.5 grams of sugar, 0.5 fiber, 64 milligrams of cholesterol, and 329 milligrams of sodium.

Recipe 7: Apple Peanut Butter Cakes combined with Stewed Cinnamon and Apple Filling

Nourish your morning protein pancake with a simple 4-ingredient baked apple filling. Servings - 8

From beginning to end - 1 hour 15 minutes

Preparation - 15 minutes cooking - 1 hour

Below are the ingredients:

- Whole wheat flour (3/4 cups)

- ¾ cups of flour

- ¼ cups of sugar

- Baking powder (1 teaspoon)

- Grounded cinnamon (1 tablespoon)

- 1½ cup of skim milk

- ½ cups of natural apple sauce (unsweetened)

- ½ cup of unsalted, raw, and creamy peanut butter

- 1 cup diced apples
- 2-3 teaspoons of unsalted butter

- Roasted cinnamon

- 1 teaspoon unsalted butter

- 1or 2 sliced apples

- Cinnamon

- Water

- Maple syrup (for serving)

How to prepare:

Whisk together the cinnamon, baking powder, sugar, and flour in a large bowl. Also, in another small bowl, whisk the apple sauce, milk, and peanut butter. Then mix the wet ingredients and the dry ingredients. Ensure everything is well mixed; however, be careful not to mix too much. Turn the apples into diced apples.

Afterward, melt the butter on a grill over medium heat. Use only enough to cover with a grill. With a measuring cup, drop the dough on the grill and level with a spatula. For another five minutes, let it cook, so that the edges have solidified, and the dough begins to bubble in the middle. Turn before baking on the other side fcr about another 4 minutes.

Repeat this method with the rest of the dough and add butter to the grill as needed. Maintain the warmth of the pancakes with the toaster oven.

How to prepare the roasted cinnamon:

Firstly, melt 1 teaspoon of butter in a pan and add cinnamon, sliced apples, and a few teaspoons of water. Secondly, cover and occasionally stir until apples are soft ard slightly caramelized. Thirdly, serve pancakes with maple syrup and toasted cinnamon.

The nutritional value is 245 calories, 9.5 grams total fat, 2 grams saturated fats, 8 grams proteins, 35 grams carbohydrates, 13 grams sugar, 4 grams fiber, 3 milligrams cholesterol, and 89 milligrams of sodium.

Recipe 8: Butternut squash and sausage risotto

This risotto is one of the very exceptional healthy ingredients. Butternut squash contaiɔs a lot of antioxidants, vitamins C, A, and E. It also comprises magnesium, potassium, and vitamin B6. Italian sausage adds tasty protein.

Serving - 6

From beginning and end - 1 hour 15 minutes

Preparation: 20 minutes cooking: 55 minutes

Below are the ingredients:
  • A medium or small-sized pumpkin (about 4-5 cups)

  • Extra virgin olive oil divided (3 tablespoons)

  • Half kilo of Italian sausage (cooked chicken and turkey 1.5

  cups) • Chopped yellow onions (half cup)

  • 1 tablespoon butter

  • Arborio rice (1 ¼ cups)

  • 4 dl vegetable or chicken broth

  • 1 cup water

  • Half cup of Parmigiano Reggiano cheese (finely grated)

- ½ cups of pecorino romano (finely grated)

- Chopped fresh sage (1 tablespoon)

- Half teaspoon salt

How to prepare:

Preheat oven to 450 degrees Fahrenheit. Place the diced and peeled pumpkin on a baking sheet. Afterward, sprinkle 2 tablespoons of olive oil on top of the pumpkin, then mix over the surface. Next, bake for 20 minutes or until soft, remove from oven.

While the pumpkin is frying, add the sausage in a large skillet over high heat. Brown the sausage until it's fully cooked, then stir for about 7-10 minutes before draining the fat. Tear the cheeses, dice the onion and sage leaves.

For the next step, add 1 tablespoon each of butter and olive oil in a large Dutch oven over medium heat. Then add chopped onion and saute until soft for about 4 to 5 minutes.

Add rice and sauté for 1 minute and begin adding the broth, one at a time. Afterward, stir the rice constantly and add the broth before adding a cup as the rice starts to soak in. Do this for about 30 minutes. When out of stock, change to water.

When the rice turns creamy, stop adding water, then add parmesan cheese and sage. Add some more water if the rice looks dry or is still crispy while it is still hot.

After the risotto has absorbed the liquid, put the pumpkin and cooked sausage. Taste and add salt if desired and serve hot.

The nutritional value per serving, 469 calories, 22 grams total fat, 17 grams proteins, 52 grams carbohydrates, 1 gram sugar, 6 grams fiber, and 682 milligrams of sodium.

Recipe 9: Black bean salad with honey-lime vinaigrette

To brown this protein- and fiber-filled salad, pack the sauce and throw it in just before eating. You can add any muscle-building protein with extra grilled chicken on top.

Servings - 8

From beginning and end - 20 minutes

Preparation - 15 minutes cooking - 5 minutes

Below are the ingredients:

- For salad
- Fresh corn (landed and cleaned)
- Rinsed & drained black beans (1 can)
- 1 can of rinsed and drained of kidney beans
- 1 yellow or red pepper seeds (cubes and stems)
- 1 green pepper seeds (cubes and stems)
- Half medium-sized red onions (diced and peeled)
- Half cup of fresh coriander leaves (coarsely chopped)
- Half jalapeno (cubes and seeds)
- 1 teaspoon Dijon mustard
- 1 lime (peeled)
- 2 tablespoons of honey
- 1/3 cup olive oil
- Sea salt

How to prepare:

The salads – First, boil the pot of water, add the corn, and bring to a boil for about 5 minutes then drain and rinse the corn under cold water. After that, pat dry, and when it has cooled enough to touch, you should cut the kernels from the cob. After that add it to the large mixing bowl.

Afterward, add jalapeno, coriander, onion, pepper, beans, and corn in the same bowl.

For the others, mix the honey, lime juice, lime peel, and mustard in a small bowl. Then beat in the olive oil.

The nutritional value, 231calories, 10 grams total fat, 1 gram saturated fats, 6 grams proteins, 31 carbohydrates, 6 grams of sugar, 6 grams of fiber, and 231 milligrams of sodium.

Recipe 10: Sweet cranberries and apple lentils

This dish is full of healthy fat, fiber, vitamin C, selenium, and iron which is essential for the health of your body.

Serving - 6

From beginning and end - 15 minutes

Preparation: 15 minutes

Below are the ingredients:

- 9 ounces of steamed lentils
- 2 diced apples
- 2 pears or other diced seasonal fruit
- 1/4 cup diced red onion
- Half cup dried cranberries
- Half cup chopped pecans
- Extra virgin olive oil (3 tablespoons)
- Balsamic vinegar stuffed with fruit (2 tablespoons)
- 2 teaspoons dried rosemary
- Black pepper

How to prepare:

First, in a medium bowl or container, mix the pears, apples and lentils, apples, pears with the pecans and cranberries. Secondly, combine the oil and balsamic vinegar together in a small bowl.

Thirdly, pour the sauce over the lentil mixture and add the rosemary and black pepper to taste.

The nutritional value per serving, 240 calories, 14 grams total fat, 1.5 grams saturated fats, 1 gram of protein, and 31 grams of carbohydrates. It also has 20 grams of sugar and 5 grams of fiber.

Recipe 11: Shrimp Paella

Since the 2015 American Dietary Recommendations confirmed that you do not have to be completely strict with cholesterol, you can once in a while enjoy delicious seafood like shrimp.

Serving - 6
From beginning to end - 1 hour 15 minutes

Preparation - 15 minutes cooking - 1 hour

Below are the ingredients:

- Coarse salt (1/4 teaspoon)

- Half teaspoon coarse black pepper

- 3/4 teaspoon peppers

- Extra virgin olive oil (5 tablespoons)

- Small boneless chicken breasts or thighs without skin (3 or 4)

- Chopped sweet Spanish onion (3/4 cups)

- 1 teaspoon ground garlic

- 1 cup of Arborio rice

- 1 cup of crushed tomatoes

- 4 cups of seafood broth or chicken

- 1 juice of whole Meyer lemon (3-4 tablespoons)

- a pinch of saffron (about 7-10 threads)

- Frozen peas (11/2 cups)

- 1 large chopped red pepper (stem, seeds, and all removed)

- 1/2 lb stripped and peeled shrimp (tails on or off)

- Chopped fresh parsley

How to prepare:

Beat ¼ teaspoon of salt, paprika, and pepper in a small bowl. Heat 3 tablespoons of olive oil with a big pan. Use a thick-bottomed pan with high sides and top. Add the chicken breast or thighs before seasoning with half the salt, paprika, and pepper mixture. When the chicken starts to show some color, turn and season with the remaining mixture and cook until it gets more color. However, do not cook thoroughly, then transfer the chicken from the pan to the plate.

Afterward, heat the remaining oil in a pan, add the onions, and saute until translucent before adding the garlic. Then fry for about a minute. Afterward, add the rice and sauté for about 30 seconds until the rice grains turn pearly. Add the crushed tomatoes, lemon juice, water, the remaining black pepper, saffron, and the remaining pepper.

After that, cover the pan and allow to cook for about 15-20 minutes. When the water is absorbed about halfway through, remove the cover without mixing the rice. Note that the crispy husk that forms on the bottom of the pan is considered a delicacy. Then add the pepper and peas and gently turn them over the rice. Avoid disturbing the rice at the bottom of the pan.

Afterward, place the chicken and shrimp on top of the rice and vegetables, then sprinkle another pinch of salt and pepper on it and replace the lid. Cook for about 10 minutes until the chicken is cooked thoroughly and the shrimp have turned pink and started to curl. Allow the remaining water and steam to cook to the end of the container. Check it after 5-10 minutes. You know it's done when the rice is tender but not sticky.

The nutritional value per serving is 591 calories, 19 grams of total fat, 3 grams of saturated fats, 51 grams of proteins, 54 grams of carbohydrates, and 9 grams of sugar. Then it offers 4 grams of fiber, 167 milligrams of cholesterol, and 719 milligrams of sodium.

Recipe 12: Maple and smoked paprika chicken

These two go well together for this easy chicken dish. Make sure the bottle reads 100% pure maple syrup when you buy maple syrup. For peppers, choose from hot and mild varieties.

Serving - 4

From beginning to end - 55 minutes

Preparation - 5 minutes cooking - 50 minutes

Below are the ingredients:

- Bone-in chicken breast fillets or split whole chicken (4)
- Olive oil (2 tablespoons)
- Pepper and sea salt
- 1 tablespoon maple syrup
- 1 teaspoon smoked peppers
- 1 teaspoon rustic Dijon
- Half teaspoon turmeric
- 1 tablespoon chopped fresh oregano chopped

How to prepare:

After preheating the oven, place the chicken skin side up in the pan. Then use a small bowl to mix maple, olive oil, oregano, paprika, salt, and pepper. The next thing to do is to rub the spice mixture over the chicken. Bake for 45 minutes then, turn the oven to fry the skin crispy for about 3-5 minutes.
The nutritional value per serving is 577 calories, 34 grams of total fat, 9 grams of saturated fats, 61 grams of proteins, and 4 grams of Carbs. It also offers 3 grams of sugar, 186 milligrams of cholesterol, and 347 milligrams of

sodium.

Recipe 13: Spanakopita Turkey Casserole

This is a protein-rich meal that offers 35 grams per serving! It is an excellent muscle building dish with quinoa, cheese, and lean turkey.

Servings - 6

From beginning to end - 1 hour 20 minutes

Preparation - 15 minutes cooking - 1 hour 5 minutes

Below are the ingredients:

- 1 cup dried quinoa

- Half chopped red onion

- 1 tablespoon grapeseed oil

- 1¼ lbs grounded 99% lean ground turkey

- 1 box of frozen spinach (melted and pressed dry)

- ¼ cups of chopped parsley

- 2 cups chicken broth

- ¾ cup of feta

- 2 eggs

- ¾ cup of4 cheese Italian mixture

- 1 tablespoon garlic

- 1 tablespoon Italian spice mix or 1/4 teaspoon oregano, basil, and

  thyme) • Half teaspoon of salt

- Half teaspoon of white pepper

How to prepare:

After preheating the oven boil Quinoa according to the instructions on the package. Replace the chicken broth with water and allow the quinoa to cool completely before using it in the pan.

Saute the red onion in the grapeseed oil for 3-4 minutes before adding the grounced turkey and saute until thoroughly cooked. Use a large bowl to mix everything, from the turkey/onion mix, eggs, spices, parsley, spinach, and chicken broth.

After that, mix well until the mixture looks good before transferring to a 9 × 13 baking dish that you've sprayed with cooking oil. Sprinkle a mixture of four slices of cheese over the pan. Afterward, bake for 40 minutes until the pan has thickened and starts to turn golden brown. Turn on the chicken before frying for about 3-4 minutes to get a beautiful crispy crust. Then allow sitting for 15 minutes before serving.

The nutritional value per serving is 375 calories, 15 grams total fat, 35 grams protein, and 15 grams carbohydrates.

Recipe 14: Cilantro Pesto Pasta with Chicken

Skip the tomato sauce and add your whole grain pasta with homemade pesto. The pesto can be made from cayenne, coriander, and walnuts.

Servings - 10

From beginning to end - 30 minutes

Preparation - 15 minutes cooking - 15 minutes

Below are the ingredients:

- 1 pound whole-grain penne pasta

- Fresh coriander (about 2 cups)

- 2 cloves of grounded garlic

- A tablespoon of white wine vinegar (you may also use lemon juice) • 1/4 cup of grated parmesan cheese

- Half teaspoon cayenne pepper

- Half cup walnuts

- Salt (1/4 teaspoon)

- 1/3 dl extra virgin olive oil

- 2 cups of boiled chicken (you can use roasted white meat to reduce calories) • 3 diced tomatoes (ripened in rum or vine)

How to prepare:

Firstly, boil in a large pot of water, add the pasta, and allow the water to boil. Cook the pasta for about 10 minutes, then drain well. Secondly, mix the garlic, coriander, parmesan cheese, lemon juice, nuts, cayenne pepper, and salt in an electric food processor or blender.
After that, add about half the amount of olive oil and stir in the pesto. Then add

the olive oil until the pesto has reached the desired composition. Next, pour the pesto into a small saucepan and heat over low heat as you stir until the pesto begins to boil.

Afterward, pour the sauce into a large bowl and add the pasta on top of the sauce before turning over to cover. Add the chicken and mix all the ingredients well. Add fresh coriander and freshly sliced tomatoes to garnish.

The nutritional value is 320 calories, 15 grams total fat, 2 grams of saturated fats, 13 grams proteins, 36 grams of Carbs, 5 grams of fiber, 15 milligrams of cholesterol, and 100 milligrams of sodium.

Recipe 15: Soy maple glazed salmon

It will likely become your everyday evening recipe after preparing this. Salmon is full of omega-3 fats that help fight inflammation, precisely for hard-working muscles.

Serving - 4

From beginning to end - 30 minutes and another 30 minutes in the

refrigerator Preparation - 15 minutes cooking - 15 minutes

Below are the ingredients:

- 1 lb wild salmon fillets
- 3 tablespoons of pure maple syrup
- Soy sauce (1/4 cups)
- Dark sesame oil (3 tablespoons)
- 2 teaspoons of Dijon, or you can use granular mustard
- Half Teaspoon of sriracha or Asian chili sauce
- 2 chopped green onions
- 2 cloves of grounded garlic
- 2 tablespoons of chopped fresh ginger

How to prepare:

In a small bowl, the first step is to mix the maple syrup, sesame oil, soy sauce, chill sauce, and mustard. Stir in the garlic, onion, and ginger. Then pour the marinade into an 8 x 8-inch oven pan before placing the salmon in the marinade with the skin side up. Let the salmon marinate for 30 minutes to an hour.

For the BBQ grill method, preheat and oil the grill lightly, then place the

salmon skin side down before closing the lid. Grill over average heat for about 15 minutes or until
white protein and fish flakes are visibleServe and Garnish with the chopped green onions and sesame seeds if desired.

The nutritional value is 274 calories, 14.2 grams total fat, 2.1 grams saturated fats, 29 grams proteins, 5 grams of carbohydrates, 4 grams of sugar, 81 milligrams of cholesterol, and 330 milligrams of sodium.

Recipe 16: Turkey meatballs

These meatballs are made out of minced turkey plus a variety of low-calorie herbs. These add a ton of flavor to the meal. Serve with your homemade tomato sauce with whole-grain pasta, or fill the pita dish with steamed escarole.

Servings - 5

From beginning to end - 40 minutes

Preparation - 20 minutes cooking - 20 minutes

Below are the ingredients:

- 3 proteins lightly beaten
- Half cup of chopped onions
- 1¼ pounds of minced turkey breast (only the meat)
- Half cup of freshly grated parmesan cheese
- Fresh chopped parsley (2 tablespoons)
- ¼ teaspoon of garlic powder
- Half cup of regular, dry breadcrumbs
- 1 teaspoon freshly ground black pepper
- 1 teaspoon of grounded garlic cloves
- 1 tablespoon dried oregano
- 1 tablespoon dried basil

How to prepare:

Firstly, preheat the oven to 450 degrees Fahrenheit. Mix all ingredients thoroughly in a large bowl. Then wet your hand with 10 meatballs by swirling between your palms. Afterward, put the meatballs in a large baking dish with a small amount of water. Secondly, cook for 20 minutes and keep an eye on the pan.

The nutritional value is 258 calories, 6 grams of total fat, 39.6 grams of proteins, 11.2 grams of carbohydrates, and 380 milligrams of sodium.

Recipe 17: Peppers stuffed with sausage and quinoa

Instead of traditional rice, you can use protein-rich quinoa and tons of chopped vegetables to fill in. This is good food to prepare on a busy weekday evening.

Servings - 6

From beginning to end - 52 minutes

Preparation - 20 minutes cooking - 32 minutes

Below are the ingredients:

- 6 red peppers
- 1 tablespoon olive oil
- 1 pack Applegate
- Diced pepper
- 2 cups peeled and diced eggplant
- 1 cup sliced mushrooms
- ¼ cups of chopped red onion
- Half teaspoon of kosher salt
- ¼ teaspoon black pepper
- 1 cup drained and rinsed cannellini beans
- 1 clove of grounded garlic
- 2 teaspoons chopped fresh thyme
- Half cup of low-sodium chicken broth
- A cup of marinade sauce
- 1 and a half cups of boiled quinoa
- Half cups of grated mozzarella cheese

How to prepare:

Preheat oven to 350 degrees, then place peppers on its side and slice the base on a flat surface. The ends of the pepper should be cut off. Then scrape the seeds before setting them aside. Then heat 1 teaspoon of oil in a pan, add the sausage, and cook until brown. Then transfer to a bowl. Afterward, heat the oil that's left in the pan and add eggplant, onion, and mushrooms. Use your salt and pepper to season the mixture, then sauté for 5 minutes until cooked thoroughly. Add your beans, thyme, ¼ cup of broth, garlic, boiled sausage, and marinade. You can continue cooking for another 2 minutes before turning off the heat and stirring in the Quinoa. Fill each pepper with Quinoa mixture before sprinkling with grated cheese.

Afterward, transfer to an oven-proof dish and pour the remaining broth into the bottom. Cover and allow to bake for 15 minutes before removing the foil. Then bake for another 10 minutes.

The nutritional value is 298 calories, 10 grams of total fat, 3 grams of saturated fats, 19 grams of proteins, 33 grams of carbohydrates, 8 grams of fiber, and 659 milligrams of sodium.

Recipe 18: Beef stew with carrots and tomatoes

Brighten up your daily stew by adding spicing it up with various flavors. This is the perfect way to make diner liven up your health regimen.

Serving - 4

From beginning to end - 2 hours 10 minutes

Preparation - 30 minutes cooking - 1 hour 40 minutes

Below are the ingredients:

- 1 tablespoon olive oil

- 2 and a half lbs boneless beef (cut into 1-inch cubes)

- 1 medium diced yellow onion

- 2 cups of unsalted chicken broth

- 2 tablespoons jerk sauce

- 2 teaspoons Jamaican allspice

- Half cinnamon

- 1 tablespoon thyme

- 2 cups of boiled brown rice or quinoa

How to prepare:

Firstly, preheat the oven to 350 degrees F and heat the olive oil in a Dutch oven over medium heat. After that, add the beef and let it cook for about 5 minutes and a half.

Secondly, stir in the beef, add carrots, onions, and garlic, and then saute for 3 minutes. Thirdly, add tomatoes, chicken broth, spices, and jerk sauce before boiling. Next, cover the Dutch oven and place it in the oven. Allow cooling for about 1 hour.
Then bring out your stew from the oven and remove the bearing leaves. Lessen over the heat if the stew is too thin. Afterward, serve over brown rice or quinoa and with greens.

The nutritional value per serving is 480 calories, 15 grams total fat, 5 grams saturated fat, 57 grams of proteins, and 19 grams of carbohydrates. It also has 2 grams of sugar, 2 grams of fiber, 131 milligrams of cholesterol, and 275 milligrams of sodium.

Recipe 19: Slow Cooker Peanut BBQ Pulled Pork Sandwiches with Thai Ginger Slawilla

Take a slow cooker out to make these mouth-watering, protein-rich pork sandwiches. You can also whisk an Asian-style salad made from lime, ginger, cabbage, peppers, and jalapeno on top of your pork.

Servings - 8

From beginning to end - 8 hours 30 minutes

Preparation - 30 minutes cooking - 8 hours

Below are the ingredients:

- 3-4 lb pork shoulder
- 1 teaspoon smoked peppers
- 1 teaspoon garlic powder
- Half teaspoon of grounded ginger
- 2 tablespoons of brown sugar
- Freshly ground pepper and sea salt
- 2 teaspoons of canola or vegetable oil
- One-third of a cup of vegetable or chicken broth
- 8 buns
- Peanut butter BBQ sauce
- ¼ cups of smooth, heated peanut butter

- ⅓ cup of ketchup

- 1 teaspoon molasses

- 1 teaspoon garlic powder

- Half teaspoon ground ginger

- 2 tablespoons Thai sweet red chili sauce
- 1 tablespoon rice wine vinegar

- 1 lime juice

- Thai Ginger Slawille

- Chopped cabbage (4 cups)

- Chopped peppers (2)

- Half jalapeno (cubes and seeds)

- ¼ cups of freshly chopped coriander

- 2 juiced limes

- 2 teaspoons of freshly grated ginger

- 1 tablespoon of Thai sweet red chili sauce

- 1 tablespoon rice wine vinegar

- Granular sweetener (1 tablespoon)

- ¼ cups of roasted honey peanuts

How to prepare:

For pork, pat it dry with kitchen paper and mix all the spices in a bowl before rubbing the meat all over. Alternatively, you can heat a large pan over medium heat and add oil. Fry the pork on each side for about 2-3 minutes per half.

Then add the pork and broth to the pan and cook for 8 hours. Afterward, prepare the BBQ sauce for about 30 minutes. It should be thick and creamy in composition. Now, once the pork is cooked, transfer it to a cutting board for cutting and removing any layers of fat/bone. Strain the remaining liquid from the pan and set it aside.

After that, add the pork back to the pan with 11 cups of strained liquid and most BBQ sauce. Let the pork rest for 20-30 minutes to absorb the juices and sauce. Then, in the meantime, prepare the salad by combining all the ingredients, except the peanuts in a
large bowl and leave it alone at room temperature to allow the flavors to mix. When ready to serve, you can sprinkle with chopped peanuts.

You can roast the rolls in a toaster oven or use a hot pan. Make a layer of pulled pork, lory BBQ sauce, and slaw, then serve!

The nutritional value is 438calories, 15 grams of total fat, 3.5 grams of saturated fats, 36 grams of proteins, and 40 grams of carbohydrates. It also contains 16 grams of sugar, 5.5 grams of fiber, 90 milligrams of cholesterol, and 598 milligrams of sodium.

Recipe 20: Chicken thigh pastries stuffed with olives and prunes

Book a package of prunes to make this tasty meal. This is so wholesome.

Servings - 8

From beginning to end - 1 hour 20 minutes

Preparation - 20 minutes cooking - 1 hour

Below are the ingredients:

- 2 cans of white rinsed and drained beans
- One and a half cups of mixed diced olives (e.g., Sicilian and Kalamata olives) • 2 tablespoons olive oil
- Prunes (half cups)
- 1½ cans of roasted diced tomatoes
- Half teaspoon grated orange peel
- Salt
- Pepper
- 2 packets of chicken thighs
- Grounded red pepper
- Italian spice

How to prepare:

Firstly, mix the beans, olives, prunes, olive oil, orange peel, tomatoes, salt, and pepper. Secondly, pound chicken thighs and flatten. Spread the tapenade mixture thoroughly on the chicken thighs. Then roll and hold it with a toothpick. Repeat with the remaining chicken pieces.

Then place in a pan and grate the remaining olive oil, ground red pepper, and

Italian spices. Afterward, cover the pan with foil before baking at 350 degrees for 1 hour. Then remove the foil and fry until brown. Serve and enjoy.

The nutritional value per serving is 242 calories, 1.5 grams of total fat, 23.7 grams of proteins, 16 grams of carbs, and 3.2 grams of fiber.

Summary

So essentially, preparing meals is all about planning meals and how to make the most of them. The great thing is that you can plan as much or as little as you want since it all depends on you. However, the critical idea in meal planning is to schedule your meals for the week and prepare them in advance. For instance, on a Monday afternoon, you sit
at a table and plan precisely what meals to eat each day of the week. Then you start preparing and storing food in advance.

That way, you'll have all your meals ready throughout the following week. You can simply reheat them when it's time to enjoy them. As you can imagine, the benefits of preparing meals are so much, making it a popular option, especially if you have a busy work schedule to maintain.

The Main Benefits

The following are the main benefits of planning and preparing your meals in advance.

1. SAVES TIME - One of the most well-known benefits of meal planning is simply saving time. Preparing all meals in advance is advantageous since bodybuilders can prepare food in bulk and store it for eating all week. There's no need to worry about making lunch or dinner every day. You have already made them at the beginning of the week. If you need to hurry or have a meeting to hold, it doesn't get affected by anything. Just bring out the prepared meal from the fridge and reheat it.

2. SAVE MONEY - You also save money by learning how to prepare meals efficiently. Simply plan your meal and get yourself the right ingredients in bulk during the weekly Grocery shopping. With the intended contents of your belly preplanned, you probably won't spend the extra money on takeaway or impulse shopping when you drive to the supermarket. When your meals are already planned, you can also do better with your budgeting.

3. CUT WASTE – Save and don't waste. Making meals a week saves time and money, which essentially leads to a significant reduction in waste. Everything you buy on a meal trip comes with a weekly calendar, and there isn't a reason for you to have any leftovers in the fridge or around you at the end of the week. All the ingredients are put in the dishes; thus, you can freeze it as a spare meal if you over-cook.

4. DOSAGE CONTROL – In the case of weight loss, preparing meals is a great option to reduce calories. Once a person prepares meals in advance, he can also dispense each meal. Such a person can divide foods into smaller meals and avoid the temptation to make all the leftovers in one sitting!

5. AVOID HUNGER – Inasmuch as there is a chance you may prepare smaller portions, still preparing weekly meals in advance will help you cut out hunger. This is because you always have your meal for the day ready. You'll never
need to go for snacks while waiting for food to cook. Also, you're not going to be tempted to take that takeaway pizza since you know that there's food, and it's good as soon as you get home.

6. PLAN YOUR RESTAURANT – As said earlier, meal preparation is healthier and easier because you can make sure each meal has what you need. Talk about the nutrients and ingredients you need for a balanced diet. Instead of just throwing whatever you see inside your belly, you should actively plan a healthy eating program. Such that will be filled with veggies, nutrients, and more.

7. BEST TIPS FOR MAKING MEALS – Simply put, the whole process becomes easier over time. Preparing a meal may appear daunting, and of course, people, from time to time, may initially notice that they have forgotten a strange meal or need to find a way to reschedule. However, making meals indeed gets easier as the design improves and you improve. The best way to improve is a no-brainer, which is to get started!

In conclusion, do not be afraid to build a table for this. You can help with your planning by creating a spreadsheet or just a simple list to help track your meal preparation.

Write down your daily meals and schedule them. This way, you allow yourself to vary your plan and ensure you're balanced and exploring a variety of diets throughout the week.

Chapter 2 – How to Improve your Health and Overall Wellness

Being a bodybuilder has its roots in the desire for wellness, so we all must understand precisely what we mean by fitness. Wellness can be defined as practicing healthy habits daily to achieve better mental and physical health outcomes. The point of this is to ensure that you not only survive, but you succeed.

To comprehend why wellness is so essential, it is vital to understand how it relates to health. According to the WHO (World Health Organization), health may be defined as a state of complete physical, social and mental wellness and not merely the absence of disease or infirmity.

Several critical areas of a person's lifestyle are regarded as dimensions of the individual's general well-being. These dimensions are 8 and cover social fitness, connection, mindfulness, nutrition, and sleep. It's pertinent also to understand that different things can impact a bodybuilder's mental and physical health. By making healthy and straightforward choices consistently and persistently, you are well on your way to reducing stress, achieving optimal well-being, and building positive social interactions.

You can start with small changes in each dimension and take it one day at a time. You don't have to do so much on a restrictive diet to achieve the desired balance that's necessary for your wholeness. Below are the 8 dimensions of wellness:

1. Emotional wellness

Emotional wellness has to do with the ability to cope effectively with life's difficulties. It is being emotionally aware and maintaining healthy relationships with yourself and the people around you. People with healthy emotional well-being are confident, have a good grasp of their behaviors and emotions, and have suitable coping mechanisms to deal with difficult situations. You need to build flexibility within yourself to allow you to overcome the barriers in your life. Emotional well-being concerns the following:

- Healthy relationships

- Resilience

- Ability to ask for help

- Awareness of feelings

- Ability to express your feelings around those you trust

- Learning your strengths
- Work on the things you want to improve

- Develop confidence in oneself

- Ability to show emotions, i.e., fear, joy, anger, sadness, happiness, frustration, gratitude, etc.

- Mental health

- Maintaining a positive self-image

2. Spiritual wellness

Being well spiritually concerns having a vision and knowing the purpose for your existence which revolves around personal values and beliefs. Spiritual health can include contact with meditation, nature, prayer, introspection, and more. Being spiritually healthy implies that you have strong a strong sense of inner peace, values, and a purpose in life. This includes:

- You spend time on activities that strengthen your sense of connection with others, nature, and yourself

- A healthy relationship with nature

- Finding principles, values, and beliefs

- Having a bigger purpose than the regular materialistic ones

- Being part of a like-minded community

- Helping other people in need

- Exploring your personal values

- Accepting others as they are

- Observing me-time, quiet time

• Religious or otherwise spiritual activities and practices

3. Mental wellness

Mental well-being is about working your mind, learning new things, as well as expanding your own skills and knowledge. Being intellectually healthy is key to your growth mentally, ability to remember, creativity, and ability to think critically.

Being mentally well means that you are:

- Using your creative abilities
- Practicing critical thinking

- Being a lifelong learner

- Taking and maintaining your interest in books, articles, and any other content • Getting to know public/community events

- Ability to concentrate on your own skills and learn new things

- Ability to examine, develop, solve problems, and more

- Ability to challenge yourself mentally through things like puzzles, learning a new instrument, learning a new language, etc.

- Maintaining a positive self-image

4. Physical wellness

Physical wellness includes nights of adequate sleep, a healthy diet, the proper amount of regular physical activity, as well as the prevention and management of diseases. Physically unhealthiness can lead to numerous health illnesses. Developing healthy lifestyles and making healthy choices will improve your overall well-being. This includes the following:

- Regular exercises

- Feeling comfortable with your body

- Constant medical check-up

- Healthy consumption of proper nutrition

- Keeping your blood pressure balanced

- Comprehending how sleep and stress can affect your health

- Stress reduction

- The development of healthy habits

- Avoid consuming cigarettes, alcohol, and other substances (or at least consume them responsibly)

- Sleeping enough

- Taking all medicines prescribed by your doctor

- Understanding your body fully

5. Environmental wellness

Environmental wellness means being in a caring and healthy environment and knowing and respecting the environment. The environment around you can significantly affect how you feel and thus your life generally. For instance, individuals living in countries with lots of rain and cloudy days may suffer from seasonal depression that can impact their social health, emotional health, mental health, e.t.c negatively. Generally, a positive environment around you and caring for your own part of the planet will help you feel more satisfied. Environmental well-being comprises the following:

- Making sure your home is clean

- Spending time outdoors

- Using environmentally friendly products

- Recycling

- Maintaining a peaceful home environment

- Community participation

- Being aware of pollution and your own contribution to it

- Being aware of the activities in your environment

6. Financial wellness

Financial well-being concerns your financial responsibilities, financial literacy, and general accountability. The struggle with finance and the uncertain economic situation is a problem that can cause a lot of stress for an individual and his family. Keeping your finances in check is vital to improving your daily life. An individual's financial well-being includes:

- Designing and maintaining your budget and tracking expenses

- Devising ways to save your money

- Being financially responsible

- Having professional financial assistance (if necessary)

- Keeping tabs on your credit information and account statements

- Knowing and improving your financial literacy

7. Occupational wellness

Well-being at work deals with a person's level of satisfaction with his vocation. This is about how enriching your profession is, regardless of whether it is actually a professional work or just your academic work. One common cause of stress for many Americans is their job and the demands associated with it. Work-life balance is extremely important for overall health and well-being. The first step to achieving this is a job you enjoy and are passionate about. It is also vital that you have a positive work atmosphere and people who support you and your goal. Well-being at work includes:

- Attaining some level of personal satisfaction from your

profession • Good balance between leisure and work and leisure

- Learning and being able to communicate and relate with your co-workers effectively

- Developing good workplace habits and work-related skills

- Discovering the career opportunities available to you or volunteer opportunities that ignite your passion

- Setting realistic career goals

- Learning and understanding your disabilities

- Challenging societal expectations and barriers

8. Social wellness

Social wellness has to do with having a solid support network and a deep sense of connection with other people in your community. It gives you a sense of belonging. Feeling isolated or lonely can lead to negative mental and physical health. The healthy relationships we have with relatives and family are essential to our well-being socially, spiritually, and emotionally. Social welfare includes:

- Joining a social group, or a volunteer group
- Focusing on the maintenance of a social connection by keeping in touch with others
- Opportunity to interact with different people and learn
- Being aware of your impact on the community
- Developing good communication skills
- Knowing and comprehending gender and gender roles and the attached stereotypes
- The ability to set and maintain boundaries
- Having a solid support network
- Developing positive relationships
- Ability to ask for help when needed

Effect of physical activity gaining weight and obesity

Several scientists have carried out many studies to try to figure out the implications of physical training on gaining weight and obesity. However, comprehensive studies have shown a negative relationship between physical activity and weight gain over time.

One pivotal study that's based on the development of obesity as a function of physical activity was carried out by the Cooper Clinic in Texas. The research studied 2501 healthy men between the ages of 22 to 55 at baseline and five years later. The results showed that daily physical activity was negatively related to weight gain during the follow-up period. It showed that people who reduced their daily physical activity gained weight significantly, while those who maintained the same activity level during the study did not gain weight. In addition, those people who increased their physical activity during the study experienced weight loss. The report revealed that daily physical activity with a metabolic rate that's 60% higher than the base metabolic rate is essential for weight loss. Thus, 45 to 60 minutes of exercises such as gardening, brisk walking, or biking may be included in a bodybuilder's daily routine to maintain the weight of middle-aged men.

Research by Gordon-Larsen focused on the relationship between walking and weight gain. The study was performed with 4,995 men and women between the ages of 18 to 30 years. The timeframe of the test ran from 2 to 15 years. After 15 years, the outcome of walking for about 30 minutes per day and weight gain appeared little. So, for every 30 minutes of walking per day, men lost about 0.25

kg per year without anything else. So there are chances that to lose more weight, you need to go for longer than 30 minutes.

One study also indicated that obesity could lead to physical inactivity, which might seem obvious, but it's actually more severe than one would naturally think. Generally, people who are obese tend to have issues about their physique which tends to prompt them to seek ways to lose weight. However, It takes a lot of determination to stay the course and work the body until results show.

Physical Exercise on Coronary Heart Disease (CHD)

For about the past 40 years, studies have shown the role of physical activity in the prevention as well as treatment of CHD. The results so far have been consistent. Also, research has it that active; sedentary people are about twice as likely to develop or die from coronary artery disease. In fact, one recent analysis reveals that 37% of CHD
deaths are due to physical inactivity. Another health problem with this result is high blood cholesterol. Nonetheless, very few physicians seem to understand the benefits of regular exercise as they seem unaware of the current recommendations for it.

It is pivotal to be aware that we're referring to all work and leisure activities, including sports, by the physical activity here. When we say exercise, we're referring to a formal type of exercise that can also include sports.

The advantages of constant exercise include improvements in myocardial contraction and electrical stability. It also consists of an increase in stroke volume when resting and during workouts, leading to a higher maximum heart rate. An individual's heart rate slows down at rest and at a submaximal heart rate. Endothelial functions are improved this way and lead to better flow-mediated expansion. Also, through exercises, the diameter and dilation capacity of the coronary arteries gets heightened. Regular exercise also impacts the tendency of the blood to clot. Practices may lead to lower inflammatory factors like C-reactive protein, plasma fibrinogen levels, and white blood cell counts.

Exercise positively impacts your skeletal muscle, the sensitivity of your liver, and adipose tissue. Given these very favorable changes, it is essential to determine the level of exercise at which they are reflected in reducing risk factors and risk of coronary heart disease.

Numerous studies have confirmed the benefits of solid exercises in reducing the risk of coronary heart disease. A survey carried out by a researcher known as Morris on British officials was one of the landmark surveys. A cohort of 17,944 British 45-65-year-old male civil servants with no coronary heart disease was prospectively studied. After 8.5 years of studying the outcomes, the cumulative incidence of coronary heart disease by age was 3.1% in men who reported that they exercised vigorously. On the other hand, 6.9% of those who did not work out constantly had to deal with CHD.

In fact, as a result of increasingly convincing epidemiological evidence and physiological tests, In 1985, ACSM (American College of Sports Medicine) disclosed a recommendation that adults should perform about 20 minutes of intense exercise 3 times per week.

Also, there is evidence that moderately intense physical activity does prevent coronary heart disease. Moderately intense physical activity can be described as an exercise that makes your heart beat faster, your breathing harder but still allows you to speak. These types of exercises are cycling, swimming, and brisk walking.

One major study on this is from the British Regional Heart Study, which started in 1978. It involved 7735 men between the ages of 40 to 59. The selection included men with or without a history of CHD from general age-sex sex registries. Exercises A standard
questionnaire was completed by the participants. The questionnaire comprises questions concerning recreational exercises and other health habits.

The outcomes after 8 years of studying these men showed that those without a history of coronary artery disease had as much as a 50% reduction in risk when compared to those who were not active. The number of first heart attacks decreased to moderate levels with the level of physical activity. Men with a history of the disease had a similar inverse
relationship to moderate activity levels. No additional benefit was observed in those who participated in the effective activities.

According to the Honolulu Heart Program, older men who perform walking exercises are less likely to suffer CHD. Data from 2678 physically fit men between the ages of 71 and 93 years showed that those who took walks no more than 0.25 miles per day for 2 to 4 years had a doubled risk of developing coronary heart disease compared to those who walked more than 1.5 miles per day. This particular study is solid because the findings were still consistent even after adjusting for age and other risk factors.

In addition to offering directed protection against CHD, working out offers indirect protection through its effects on other risk factors. These risk factors are diabetes, high cholesterol, and high blood pressure.

• Blood pressure

The risk of CHD is directly related to both systolic and diastolic blood pressure levels. The prevailing study has it that an estimated 13% of CHD deaths are due to hypertension. Other random research based on the effects of different workout intensities and the impact on blood pressure suggests that moderate to severe intensity may cause a similar decrease in diastolic blood pressure. In addition, moderately intense exercise lowers systolic blood pressure even more than intense exercise. Moderate activity is sufficient to lower blood pressure in normotensive individuals and may therefore be helpful in the primary prevention of blood pressure.

• Diabetes

Diabetes significantly raises the odds of a person having CHD. About 3% of adults are now diagnosed with diabetes, and an estimated 2% have undiagnosed diabetes. It is believed that workouts have a significant role to play in the prevention and treatment of type 2 diabetes. This is so much the case for people who are obese or impaired glucose tolerance patients.

For instance, a Study by Nurses Health looked at the relationship between overall exercises and the risk of diabetes; then, they compared the benefits of strenuous activity and walking. This particular research looked at 70102 women aged 40 to 65 years that do not have diabetes, cancer, or CHD. The outcome showed that the relative risk of
developing diabetes decreased as total physical activity increased over the 8-year follow up period.

This risk reduction also tallies consistent intense and moderately intense workouts; this included walking. As a result, the risk reduction is related to total energy consumption.

Regular moderate physical activities such as endurance and resistance workouts are also helpful in the treatment of type 2 diabetes. Mild to moderate exercises are sufficient to control blood glucose and increase insulin sensitivity. The effect is maintained for up to 72 hours after the activity. Simply put, physical activity is a significant underutilization in the treatment of type 2 diabetes.

- Overweight & obesity

People that are obese or overweight have an increased risk of developing vascular diseases, especially CHD. Obesity has increased in this era, while average food intake has apparently declined. Thus, the entire problem seems to be based on a general decline in physical activity, which means that working out is a crucial factor in treating and preventing obesity.

Continuous and persistent physical exercise is essential for long-term weight loss and its subsequent maintenance. The beneficial mechanisms behind this are related to the increase in total energy expenditure. Another advantage is the maintenance of lean mass and the increase in metabolism.

Several studies have shown that overweight but fit people are at lower risk than those who are heavy and still in poor condition. This suggests that workouts may compensate for some of the health risks associated with obesity. One review that summarizes the epidemiological evidence indicates that the health risks of obesity are mainly under control if a person is physically active and physically fit.

- Cholesterol

The risk of CHD is directly related to blood cholesterol levels. It is estimated that 45 percent of deaths in men resulting from the disease are due to elevated blood cholesterol levels. Working out has many beneficial effects on several aspects of the blood lipid profile. For example, a single workout can improve the blood lipid profile for several days. Exercise has also been shown to reduce elevated triglyceride levels.

Exercise and Skeletal Health

As a bodybuilder, you are probably aware of the many benefits of exercise, ranging from improving muscle strength & endurance, decreasing the likelihood of having heart disease & stroke, to preventing obesity. The importance of regularly working your body so as to build and maintain healthy bones may not be as well understood. In fact, inactivity causes bone loss!

Aging, along with specific diseases and medications, can cause bone loss and fragility over time leading to a condition referred to as osteoporosis. It often occurs in men when we get old. This bone-thinning disease puts people at greater risk of breaking bones, which can severely limit mobility as well as independence.

People tend to lose muscle as they age (a disease referred to as sarcopenia). Those who suffer from osteoporosis or sarcopenia are considered weak and are more likely to fall and break a bone.

Exercise affects the bones in the same way as the muscles as it makes them stronger. Training is vital for building strong bones at a younger age and is essential for maintaining bone strength at an older age. Since your bones are living tissue, they change over time due to the forces acting on them. When bodybuilders workout regularly, your bone adapts by building more bone and thickening. However, it is essential also to note that this bone healing requires good nutrition, including adequate calcium and vitamin D.

Another benefit of the exercise is that it improves balance and coordination. This becomes especially important as we age as it helps prevent falls and possible fractures.

Exercises for strong bones

There are several forms of exercise, and all of them offer health benefits. The two most effective types for building solid bones are strength training and weight training. Exercises to improve bone strength are site-specific. For instance, walking can improve bone strength in the legs and spine, but not in the wrist.

Stretching and strengthening the posture can help prevent or reduce the upper back depression seen in many older people. Leaning on to tie shoes or sweeping and wiping can lead to spine fractures in people at high risk of a spine fracture. Try to maintain a good back position in all your activities.

1. The Weight-bearing exercise

Carrying weight describes any activity you do with your feet that pushes bones and muscles against gravity. As your feet and legs have your body weight, the bones are put under more strain, causing the bones to work harder. With weight-bearing exercise after young adulthood can help prevent further bone loss and strengthen bones.
The following are some weight-bearing exercises you can try:

- Brisk walking & hiking
- Jogging/running
- Dancing
- Jump rope

- Tennis
- Badminton
- Ping pong/pickleball
- Team sports like soccer, rugby, basketball, and volleyball
- Climbing stairs

More effective activities such as jogging and skipping rope increase bone weight and offer more bone-strengthening advantages. However, people who are debilitated or have already been diagnosed with bone thinning should discuss the appropriate types of physical activity with their doctors.

2. Strength training

In strength training exercises, resistance is added to the movement, which will force the muscles to work harder, thereby strengthening as time goes on. So even as resistance exercises focus on increasing muscle mass, they also strain and build bones.

Some well-known strength training workouts are free weights and weight machines. There are also weight training activities that require the use of your own body weight. Elastic bands can also be used to increase resistance to exercise. The general concept of workouts such as this is to exercise each major muscle group at least twice every week. However, you should endeavor to get some rest between the exercises.

3. Some other type of workout

Non-impact exercises e.g., yoga and tai chi are not as practical at strengthening bones. However, they offer significant balance training and flexibility. Other activities such as biking, swimming, and chair exercises, are not known to help with bone density. However, they are excellent alternatives to the muscles and strengthen the lungs and heart. If you have a musculoskeletal system disease, such as arthritis, that does not allow you to engage in weight-bearing activities; these workouts are good options.

An effective exercise program for bone health comprises 30 minutes of weight-bearing activity for 4 days or more in a week. In order to maintain motivation, choose an activity you like so that when fatigue sets in, you have some passion for keeping you going for longer. Essentially, you should do your best to engage in as many activities that will get you on your feet, moving around as possible.
There's no need to insist on completing the 30-minute workout at once. Since

this activity can be divided into shorter intervals if necessary. A 10-minute brisk walk thrice a day is a great way to kick-start the process. If walking outdoors isn't safe, walking all over the house and stairs-climbing are some great weight-bearing exercises.

In order to get as much benefit from workout, you need to add flexibility and balance training to your mix. All practices should end with stretching. Increasing flexibility improves your ability to move easily, can lessen your risk of injury, and provides mental relaxation.

Before choosing an operation, it is essential to consider the risk of falling. Your doctor and physiotherapist can help you plan your exercise program. Severely osteoporotic men should be careful to avoid weight lifting with their arms in an upright position. One good rule of thumb is 10-20 pounds. Such people are to also avoid exercises that bend or twist the spine. Likewise, Contact sports are not the best options for those with severe osteoporosis. Chair and corner wall exercises may be a safer option to try out.

It also has to be said that building solid bones starts from infanthood. The most appropriate time to build bone density is during the years of rapid growth. Humans are basically developing a skeleton that will last a lifetime when between the ages of 10 and 18 years old. The peak time to build density and strength is when you're in your twenties.

Weight-bearing training in adolescence is essential to achieve maximum bone strength. Physical activity for a teenager should include 20-30 minutes of weight bearing exercise for a minimum of 3-4 days a week.

When a person is 25 years old (more or less), physical activity alone will no longer be able to increase bone mass dramatically. In adults, bone density may increase by 1-2%, but this increase occurs only in the stressed skeletal area, and this improved density will disappear if the load is stopped. Still, exercise can prevent or slow bone loss and maintain muscle mass. It also preserves and strengthens the surrounding bone, as well as reducing the risk of falling. Men also need good nutrition such as calcium and vitamin D to maintain bone mass.

Middle-aged men may need hormonal supplements (estrogens or androgens) to improve or maintain bone mass as they continue to age. However, these hormones are not usually recommended for older people. Typically, for older people with significantly impaired bone, they may try bone-preserving or bone-building drugs.

For elderly adults, falls often lead to fractures that have long-term consequences, including permanent disability. The most common fractures in older people occur in the wrist, hip, and spine.

Balance training and Tai chi have been known to reduce falls by 47% and reduce the risk of hip fractures by about 25 percent. In addition, men who engage in intense physical workouts generally have a lower risk of developing a hip fracture.

When individuals lose weight, they also lose bone. Low weight at any age is associated with a higher risk of fractures and bone problems.

So, although exercise has been shown to have apparent bone-building effects in kids and adolescents and bone-preserving effects in adults, it is only one part of an overall program to prevent bone loss and reduce the risk of fractures.

It is essential to understand your individual risk of osteoporosis, such as genetic factors and family history. A balanced, calcium-rich diet, adequate vitamin D, and a healthy lifestyle (avoiding excessive alcohol and nicotine) are also important ingredients for lifelong bone health.

28 Health and Nutrition Tips that are truly Evidence based

It is effortless to become confused when it comes to your nutrition and health. The qualified experts often seem to have conflicting opinions, which can make it challenging to figure out what you should do to optimize your health. However, despite all the disagreements and conflicting reports, all sides have confirmed specific tips to aid health and nutrition. The following are 28 health and nutrition tips that are scientifically proven:

• Limit the intake of sugary drinks

Sugar-based beverages are the primary source of added sugar in the American diet. These beverages are fruit juices, soft drinks, and sweetened teas. The problem with added sugar is that multiple scientific findings have proven that these drinks increase people's probability of getting type 2 diabetes and heart disease. Also, this is true even in people who don't have excess fat.

Sugar-sweetened beverages are also uniquely harmful to children because they can contribute not only to childhood obesity but also to diseases that usually only develop into adulthood. Such conditions include non-alcoholic fatty liver and high blood pressure.

Seeing that most beverages that are out there are harmful, are there healthy options out there? Yes, and some of them are water, mineral water, unsweetened teas, and coffee.

• Take seeds and nuts

Certain people, including some bodybuilders, do not like to take nuts. This is because they are high in fat. Nonetheless, nuts and seeds are unbelievably nutritious to your body. Nuts are full of fiber, protein, and a host of minerals and vitamins and minerals that do your body nothing but good.

Also, nuts can help an individual lose weight and also reduce the possibility of having illnesses. These could either be type 2 diabetes or heart disease.

In addition, an extensive observational study revealed that a low intake of nuts and seeds might be linked to the likelihood of dying from heart disease, stroke, or type 2 diabetes. So, folks, you really need to fall in love with this nutritious food.

• Avoid ultra-processed foods

As you probably know, ultra-processed foods are foods that are full of ingredients that have been significantly modified from their original form. These sorts of foods often contain additives like the added sugar we discussed earlier, salt, colors, artificial sweeteners, highly refined oil, preservatives, and flavors. Examples of these kinds of foods are frozen foods, snacks/cakes, fast food, and chips.

Ultra-processed foods are very enjoyable in the mouth; after all, many things have been added to make them appealing. This means that it's easy to fall in love with eating them since they activate the reward areas in your brain. Thus, this leads many people to excessive calorie intake and weight gain. Studies show that diets high in ultra processed foods can contribute to obesity, heart diseases, type 2 diabetes, as well as other chronic diseases.

In addition to low-quality ingredients such as inflammatory fats, processed grains, and added sugar, these foods tend to be low in protein, fiber, and micronutrients which are much needed by your body. Thus, they provide mostly empty calories.

• Take coffee but in moderation.

We love coffee, and although it is generally considered to contain many nutrients, it is nonetheless controversial. It is rich in antioxidants certainly, and some scientists have even linked coffee consumption to longevity and a lessened probability of developing type 2 diabetes, Alzheimer's, and Parkinson's diseases, among other diseases. However, moderation is necessary when it comes to coffee.

The recommended intake appears to be 3 to 4 cups daily. It is best to consume coffee and all caffeine-based products in moderation. Excessive caffeine intake can lead to health problems that no one wants to entertain. Such health problems include palpitations and insomnia. If you're going to enjoy your coffee safely and healthily, keep your drinks under 4 cups per day. Also, avoid sugary addictives and high-calorie such as sweetened cream.

• Eat fatty fish

Fish is an excellent source of high-quality fat and healthy protein. This is quite true for fatty fish, i.e., salmon, which is full of anti-inflammatory omega-3 fatty acids and many other nutrients.

Research has proven that people who regularly eat fish have a lower risk of developing several diseases like dementia, heart disease, and inflammatory bowel disease.

• Make sure you sleep

There's no way to overemphasize the importance and necessity of good quality sleep. Poor sleep can cause insulin resistance and interfere with your appetite hormone function. It can also impair your mental and physical performance.

In addition, poor sleep is one of the most vital individual risk factors for obesity and weight gain. Individuals who fail to get enough quality sleep tend to make more dietary choices that include fat, calories, and sugar. This can result in unwanted weight gain.

• Eat intestinal bacteria

Intestinal bacteria, generally termed intestinal macrobiotics, are essential for overall health. The bacterial intestinal disorder has been linked to certain chronic diseases, like obesity and countless other digestive problems.

Good ways to improve intestinal health include eating probiotic foods like yogurt/sauerkraut, taking probiotic supplements, and plenty of fiber (when needed). Fibre mainly acts as a food source for your intestinal bacteria.

• Always stay hydrated

Hydration is a meaningful yet frequently overlooked sign of deteriorating health. Hydration helps ensure that your body functions optimally and that your blood supply is adequate. Taking water is the best method to stay hydrated since it is free of sugar, calories, and additives. Although there isn't an exact amount that everyone needs in a day, endeavor to constantly drink enough to quench your thirst.

• Do not eat heavily charred meat.

Meat can be a healthy and nutritious part of your diet. After all, it is very high in protein as well as being a rich source of nutrients. Still, problems occur when meat is burned or charred. This carbonization can result in the formation of harmful compounds. These toxic substances may increase your risk of developing certain cancer types.

Therefore, when cooking your meat, endeavor not to char or burn it. In addition, limit the consumption of processed and red meats, like lunch & bacon. This is because they are associated with an overall risk of cancer and a chance of colon cancer.

• Avoid bright light before going to bed.
When exposed to bright light in the evening before bed, it can interfere with your body's ability to produce the hormone melatonin. This is because the bright lights contain wavelengths of blue light, which prohibit such.

Some ways to reduce exposure to blue light are to use blue-light-blocking glasses. This is especially advisable for people that use a computer or other digital display for long periods. Also, it is advisable to avoid digital displays 30 minutes to an hour before bedtime.

Doing this will naturally help your body produce better melatonin as the evening progresses. This will lead to better sleep at night.

• Take vitamin D as needed

Many persons do not get enough vitamin D into their systems. Although these widespread vitamin D deficiencies are not immediately harmful, maintaining adequate vitamin D levels may improve your health by improving bone strength, lessening symptoms of depression, reducing the risk of cancer, and strengthening your immune system. For people who do not stay in the sunshine, their vitamin D levels may be low.

If you have access, it's a good idea to test your levels so you can correct your levels with vitamin D when necessary.

• Eat plenty of fruits & vegetables.

Fruits & vegetables are filled with minerals, vitamins, prebiotic fibers, and antioxidants, many of which provide powerful health effects.

Studies have revealed that people who eat more fruits and vegetables tend to live longer and lower the risk of developing obesity, heart disease, and other diseases.

• Eat enough protein

Adequate protein consumption is vital for optimal health. This is because it provides the raw materials your body needs, such as new tissues and cells.

In addition, this nutrient is essential for maintaining a reasonable weight. A high protein intake can speed up your metabolism and burn calories while you feel full. Also, it has proven to reduce cravings and the desire to eat a snack late at night.

• Stay on the move

Aerobic exercise as well as cardio is one of the most resourceful ways to stay physically and mentally healthy. It's especially effective in reducing belly fat, a harmful type of fat that accumulates around the organs. Reduced belly fat can lead to significant improvements in metabolic health.

The American Physical Activity Guidelines recommend a minimum of 150 minutes of moderate-intensity activity each week.

• Minimize or quit smoking or the use of drugs/alcohol
Smoking, alcohol, and the use of harmful drugs can all have serious health effects. If you are taking any of these actions, consider reducing or stopping them from reducing your risk of chronic illness. Speak to the doctor for more about your issue.

• Take advantage of extra virgin olive oil.

This type of olive oil is one of the healthiest vegetable oils you can find anywhere. It is full of heart-healthy monounsaturated fats and active antioxidants containing anti inflammatory properties.

This nutrition can benefit the health of your heart, as there is some evidence that people who use it have a lower risk of dying from strokes and heart attacks.

• Minimize sugar intake

Added sugar is ubiquitous in everyday foods and beverages. High intake is associated with obesity, heart disease, and even type 2 diabetes.

According to the American Dietary Recommendations, you should keep your added sugar intake below 10% of your daily caloric intake. However, WHO recommends reducing your added sugars to less than 5% of your daily calories for optimal health.

• Limit purified carbohydrates

Not all carbs are created equal. The purified carbohydrates are highly processed to remove fibers. They are relatively low in nutrients and can harm your health if eaten too much. Most ultra-processed foods are made from refined carbohydrates such as white flour, processed corn, and added sugars.

Studies show that a diet rich in processed carbohydrates may be associated with weight gain, overeating, and chronic diseases. These chronic diseases include heart disease and type 2 diabetes.

• Balance your consumption of saturated fats

Saturated fat has been controversial and was previously believed to be a significant cause of heart disease. While it's factual that saturated fat raises cholesterol levels, it also increases good cholesterol (HDL) and reduces harmful cholesterol particles. Saturated fats are associated with a lower risk of heart disease.

New research has questioned the link between saturated fats and heart disease intake. It appears that saturated fats may not affect overall health or maybe slightly positive inasmuch as the diet is nutritionally balanced and healthy.

• Lift heavyweights

Strength and resistance training are the best exercises you can use to improve your body composition and strengthen your muscles.
It may also result in significant improvements in metabolism, an increase in your metabolic rate, or the calories you burn at rest. It also helps to improve insulin sensitivity. This insulin sensitivity means your blood sugar is easier to control.

If you don't have weights, you can use your own weight or the resistance bands to have that resistance. This will produce a comparable workout with many of the same benefits. The American Physical Activity Guidelines advise that people exercise resistance training twice a week.

• Avoid artificial trans fats.

Artificial trans fats are harmful, manufactured fats that are strongly associated with inflammation and heart disease. It should be much easier to avoid them now that they are completely banned in the U.S and multiple nations. Be aware that you may still have to deal with some foods that contain small amounts of naturally occurring trans fats but do not have the same adverse effects as artificial trans fats.

• Consume plenty of herbs and spices

Today we have a variety of herbs & spices, more than ever. Not only do they provide flavor, but they can also provide several health benefits. For instance, turmeric and ginger both have potent anti-inflammatory and antioxidant effects. This may help improve your overall health.

As a result of their powerful potential health benefits, bodybuilders should strive to include a wide variety of herbs and spices in their diet.

• Take care of your social relationships.

Social relationships with friends, relatives, and loved ones you care about are essential for your mental well-being and your physical health. Hard to believe?

Well, it's true.

Studies show that people with close friends and family are healthier and live much longer than those without.

- Monitor your meals from time to time

This here is the point of it all. The only way to know precisely how many calories you eat is to weigh your food and monitor your nutrition. Monitoring your meals can also provide information about your protein intake, micronutrients, and fiber.

Although some studies have found a link between calorie monitoring and eating disorders, there is proof to suggest that people following a diet tend to be more successful in losing weight and maintaining weight loss.

- Get rid of excess belly fat.

Excess belly fat, or visceral fat, is a uniquely harmful type of fat distribution associated with an increased risk of cardio-metabolic diseases. i.e., heart diseases and type 2 diabetes.
For this reason, the size of your waist and the ratio of your waist to your hips can be much more vital signs of health than your weight.

Cutting processed carbs, eating more fiber and protein, and reducing stress are all strategies that can help you get rid of belly fat.

- Avoid restrictive diets

Diets are essential, but that alone is not entirely effective in the long run. Past weight loss is believed to be one of the strongest predictors of future weight gain.

This is because overly restrictive diets actually lower your metabolism or the number of calories you burn, making it harder to lose weight. At the same time, they also cause changes in the feeling of hunger and satiety hormone activity, which makes you hungry. They can also lead to a severe desire for foods that are high in sugar, fat, and calories.

All of this is a recipe for regenerative weight gain or what is known as a "yo-yo" weight loss. Instead of losing weight, try to adopt a healthier lifestyle. Focus on nourishing your body instead of preventing it. Weight loss should follow when you switch to whole, nutritious foods.

- Eat whole eggs

Despite the constant back and forth between eggs and health, there is a myth that eggs are harmful to you because of their cholesterol content. Studies show that they have little effect on blood cholesterol in most people and are a great source of protein and nutrients.

In addition, a review of 263,938 people found that eating an egg was not associated with a risk of heart disease.

- Meditate

Stress harms health. It can affect your dietary choices, blood sugar level, weight, susceptibility to diseases, fat distribution, etc. c. For this reason, it is essential to find healthy ways to manage your stress.

Meditation is one such method and has scientific evidence to support its use in stress management and health improvement. One research that involved 48 people with high blood pressure/type 2 diabetes showed that meditation helped lower bad cholesterol (LDL) and inflammation, especially when compared to the control group. In addition, participants in the meditation group reported improved mental and physical health.

The Best Food to take Before and After Training

Maintaining a fantastic body after exercise is by combining regular exercise with healthy foods and also eating at the right time. As a bodybuilder, feeding your body before and after each workout is essential for lots of favorable results. This includes burning calories, building muscle mass, maintaining alertness, speeding recovery, and losing. Therefore, you need to eat before training and after training.

When you train on an empty stomach, you are not giving yourself the level of energy it needs during intense training. In addition, studies have shown that you can actually cause muscle loss if you exercise regularly on an empty stomach. This is so since, whenever a person becomes hungry, his or her body goes into survival and absorbs protein from the muscles instead of the kidneys and liver. When this happens, your muscle mass will start to drop and eventually slow down your metabolism. This is not good for most people on a weight loss program. However, if your workout is just brisk walking or light jogging, an empty stomach is good. All such a person has to do is drink a glass of water before leaving the door. If you want to train more intensely, eat easily digestible carbohydrates.

The following are the best foods you can eat an hour before your workout:

Bananas: Bananas are known as the Natural Power-Barina. They are full of digestible carbohydrates as well as potassium to help maintain nerve and muscle function. Your body doesn't store potassium for very long, so an average banana is highly recommended in the morning before a workout; it helps keep your nutrient levels high. After eating the bananas, wait 30 minutes and then go to the gym.

- Oatmeal (moderately taken with berries)

- Apple & walnuts (with moderation)

- Multi-grain biscuits (with moderation)

- Sweet potatoes (take with steamed or salted broccoli in olive

oil) • A slice of toast

- A cup of fruit cocktail (washed with a glass of water)

The best pre-workout foods should comprise a sort of complex carbs and protein to keep you alert during your workout; not, make you feel pale or exhausted. Therefore, you need to eat after exercise.

Of course, you know how important it is to freshen up with the right food after an intense workout. It helps muscles grow faster and recover quickly. During exercise, your body utilizes nutrients stored in your muscles known as glycogen as an energy source. The muscles are therefore depleted of their glycogen stores and break down. You can eat or drink something that combines carbohydrates and protein from 30 minutes to an hour after a workout. This replenishes energy stores and builds/repairs broken muscles. It also helps you keep your metabolism strong and faster.

Thus, below are some foods you can eat after your workout to speed your recovery:

Protein: The source of the protein does not matter, be it eggs, milk, beans, meat, etc. Make sure the foods are not processed but organic products to allow for an excellent source of protein.

- Drink a milkshake: Do these within 60 to 90 minutes of a workout with milk, vitamins, or water. You can follow it up with an authentic meal of protein and starchy carbohydrates within 90 minutes.

- Cereals: Multigrain bread (2 slices) with brown rice, raw peanut butter, or look for other sources of cereal to soothe your taste.

- Individuals can attempt different things: For example, you can take an amino acid supplement or any fruit at your fingertips if you don't have accessories on hand. It is essential to know your body when creating a personal refueling strategy. As a bodybuilder, you can try many types of food in terms of protein, carbohydrate, vitamin, etc. Regardless of what you select for your exercise diet plan, remember that the amount of food should be proportional to the calories you consume during the day. Exercise meals don't unknowingly drive you to extra calories, resisting weight loss efforts.

Ways to Maintain a Healthy Body and Mind

The whole purpose of working out is to develop the mind and body. Superfoods are rich in nutrients and promote good health and general well-being. Not only do they improve the person's immune system, but they also contain body-healing compounds. Also, they reduce inflammation and can kill harmful bacteria. You should also know that people who regularly eat superfoods are healthier and leaner.

Clearly, as a bodybuilder, your happiness and success depend on you being in the best possible health, both in mind and body. The great news is that incorporating these superfoods into your routine can help you achieve that. Here we'll be looking at some superfoods that can help you live a more productive, longer, and healthier life.

- Avocados: This monounsaturated fruit promotes healthy blood circulation and brain health. This can lower blood pressure, which reduces the chance of cognitive impairment.

- Beans: Beans are a great source of fiber and iron and can keep your cholesterol levels at balanced levels while also lowering your risk of heart disease. It also lessens your odds of getting cancer and keeps your body humming longer.
Scientific research has shown that those who eat beans regularly weigh 7 pounds less and have a thinner waist than their peers who abstain from beans.

- Berries: It does not actually matter what kind of berries you eat as they are all full of fiber, compounds, and antioxidants that when consumed regularly. It also helps to maintain a strong mind and body. Blueberries can help improve memory and reduce the effects of dementia and Alzheimer's disease. A mere cup of strawberries contains all-day vitamin C, which contains skin firming properties.

- Broccoli: This green vegetable is full of bone-healthy vitamins such as vitamins A, C, and K and can suppress tumor growth and reduce the overall risk of cancer.

- Dark chocolate: You should consume this moderately. Taking no more than an ounce a day is enough. Dark chocolate is full of antioxidants and natural stimulants that can improve concentration, improve mood, and concentration.
- Fish (the oily variety): Both sardines, as well as salmon, are full of omega-3 fatty acids, which are unbelievably crucial to brain function and even contain substances that fight inflammation that causes nasty illnesses.

- Oranges: We all understand that oranges contain lots of vitamin C. However, some may not know that vitamin C is crucial in producing white blood cells and antibodies that are effective against infections.

- Quinoa: Quinoa is considered one of the best eating foods and is full of iron, protein, and fiber and can help control weight, prevent diabetes and reduce the risk of heart disease.

- Spinach & kale: Spinach has the ability to form healthy new cells and is a rich source of minerals, vitamins, and fiber. And studies have shown that kale can reduce the risk of ovarian, breast cancers.

- Sweet potatoes are rich in vitamin A, which strengthens the immune system and eye and bone health.

- Tea: There is something that prompts many malls in the U.S to have a new tea store. This is because tea can reduce the risk of Alzheimer's, cancer, and diabetes. Tea contains high-quality antioxidants called flavonoids. It also promotes healthier gums, bones, and teeth. In addition, it promotes positive moods. Get the most out of your freshly brewed tea while it's hot or iced.
- Tomatoes: Tomatoes offer something that's quite hard to get from any other food, which is Lycopene. This is because tomatoes can help protect the skin from lower cholesterol, UV rays and even prevent some cancers.

  - Yogurt: Yogurt contains good bacteria for intestinal health and lessens intestinal diseases. Also, because it is so rich in calcium, it helps prevent osteoporosis.

Summary

Many health problems, especially at this age and time, can interfere with varying aspects of your life. Even the minor ones can also interfere with your life. Relatively minor health problems, like indigestion, pains, and aches. It can also affect your happiness and stress levels. The best method for people to improve their ability to cope with stress and improve their well-being is to commit to healthier habits.

The truth is poor health habits can add stress to your life and also negatively impact the human capacity e to cope with stress. Stress due to poor health is significant. Health challenges also affect the rest of your life. Health problems may also end up making your daily tasks more challenging. It can also cause financial stress and even jeopardize your ability to earn a living.

Therefore, it is critical to watch what you eat and ensure that what you put in your body is healthy and that you're doing it for the right reasons.

Instead of eating right for only the desire to look more appealing in your jeans, you should also commit to eating foods that increase your energy levels and keep your body functioning. This is so since whatever you eat can affect your short and long-term health. However, it can also affect your stress levels.

It is much harder to cope with stress if you are hungry or malnourished. Hunger can make individuals more emotionally responsive to stressors. This can make you irritable or even angry in the face of small daily disturbances.

Here, let's take a look at some of the immediate consequences of a poor diet are:

- You may become sleepy regularly
- You may become nervous constantly
- You could become moody
- You'll be tired regularly
- You may discover that you're always hungry
- You could find that you are periodically weak

So has been proven repeatedly that eating well has significant long-term consequences. However, it can also help you feel more energetic and optimistic even in the short term.

Another thing that bodybuilders also need to be conscious of is the fact that finding the proper workout for you is essential. We've all heard advice on eating right and exercising, but it can be hard to fit into an exercise around a busy schedule. This is especially true when you're feeling tired from stress. One effective strategy to make exercise a regular part of your life is to build an exercise habit around your other practices. This can be done either by incorporating exercise into your morning routine, your lunch habits, or you can make it a regular part of your evening. Whichever way it goes, you need to get your psyche interested in exercises.

For instance, if you take a morning run as part of your preparation for work, it's much more likely to see to it than if you wait until when you feel like jogging. This is more the case if you live a busy life like most people today and are tired at the end of the day.

Another important way to make training easier is to choose a hobby you really like. Some examples are listening to an audiobook, walking, or attending a course at a gym where good music raises your energy levels. Finding an activity you like means you're more likely to stick with it.

Chapter 3 – Body and Sex Drive for Bodybuilders

The issue of bodybuilding concerning what your sex life should be like has always been a conflicting topic to many and for ages. Most likely, you've thought of how to balance enjoying sex with your ability to gain muscle at the gym. If so, you are not alone. Many people wonder if regular bedroom activity is something that really hampers their progress, and some are even willing to make sacrifices if that's true.

Now, although it is quite true that there is a connection between sex and muscle building, it is necessary to comprehend what this connection is entire.

Perhaps one of the most critical links between sex and muscle building is the state of zinc in the individual's body. You should know that whenever a man has an orgasm, zinc is released in the semen. This element is a critical nutrient needed for proper sperm growth and development, and when amounts fall below, infertility often becomes an issue.

In addition to this, zinc also plays an essential role in muscle development since it is inextricably linked to total testosterone levels. When there are little zinc levels in the body, it is more likely that sexual desire will be significantly reduced, as will the difficulty of producing more lean muscle mass. Therefore, zinc is lost through orgasm. If you frequently have sex but don't replace this lost zinc in your diet, you'll likely run into some kind of zinc deficiency.

To prohibit this from occurring and to ensure that you maintain a healthy libido level and move towards your goal of building muscle, you should fill your diet with foods containing a lot of zinc. This includes seafood, oysters, liver, wheat germ, pine nuts, cashew nuts, and pecans.

Another essential thing to consider is your power level when thinking about sex and muscle building. If you are very observant, you'll find that many men find that right after intercourse, they feel quite relaxed which in turn leads to asleep.

The reason for this is that after releasing semen during sex, your body has a very high release of oxytocin. This really relaxes you and can make you feel a little weaker than before sex. However, this relaxation phase does not last long and will return to normal hormone levels in your body. But then, this is not really an issue since you are not trying to practice immediately after sexual intercourse.

If it happens that you ended up having sex just around the time that you'd have liked to work out, then it is best to schedule yourself. It is advisable to aim for at least a 3-4 hour period after sexual intercourse so that the hormones can return to normal and you can regain your strength and energy.

Effects of sex on overall testosterone levels
When you consider the effects of testosterone and zinc, another correlation that needs to be considered is the overall effect of repetitive sexual activity on testosterone and libido levels. Many men think that the more often they have sex, the higher their libido. If, for some reason, a significant break is taken, libido first increases, but over time, if release is not achieved, levels may begin to decline.

Specific tests have also shown that when testosterone levels are elevated in the body, it positively affects libido levels. Therefore, when testosterone levels are higher, this, in return, keeps you interested in sex, and sex acts as positive reinforcement and maintains circulation even further. Since testosterone levels are one of the most important predictors of muscle growth and development, higher levels in the body help increase muscle growth.

Obviously, the exercises need to be done together to simulate a muscle growth response, but doing everything possible to maintain high testosterone will help you.

Sex and Concentration

Finally, the last effect of sex on muscle building is related to your concentration level. Maintaining concentration both at the gym and outdoors for actual gym workouts is critical to achieving optimal results. In some extreme cases, if you are too attached to sexual activity, you can prioritize it before regular exercise, which will significantly impact the overall results you experience.

Obviously, this is extreme, and most people have no trouble maintaining an average balance between the two. Still, if you feel like you might be pushing the line between an unhealthy balance, it's worth considering seriously.

For many people, this is never a problem. After all, their training is directly related to their desire to become more sexually attractive because they train predominantly to look good in the eyes of members of the opposite sex. So by staying in their workouts on a regular basis, they help promote opportunities for recurring intercourse.

So the next time you notice the impact of questionable sex on muscle building, keep these points in mind. The good news is, the people participating more actively in regular exercise and following a good diet are much more likely to be healthy and thus experience fewer sexual problems. The sexual issues that are prohibited include premature ejaculation or erectile dysfunction. Therefore, there's no need to be anxious about either of those affecting your overall ability to perform in bed.

As is the way of the world, in life, balance is vital, and as long as the balance is achieved, you shouldn't have to worry about maintaining a healthy sex life. This is true even as you spend your time and efforts building muscles at the gym.

Abstinence from sex before a big event

It is well known that many professional athletes and sportsmen like football players, soccer players, baseball players, martial artists, and endurance athletes have all claimed to abstain from all forms of sex and even masturbation in preparation for some big event. There is the belief that it somehow reduces an athlete's power, stamina, and strength.

This seems to be valid for a moment. However, when the athletes abstained from ejaculation for 6 days, their levels had not changed. Only on the seventh day did testosterone levels rise by 50%.

This returned to the previous level on the 8th day of abstinence. In bodybuilding, this seems to be a fragmented problem. Some professional bodybuilders don't have sex in the days or weeks before a big show like Mr. Olympia because they think it will reduce testosterone or at least eliminate their laser-like focus on the reward.

Still, Arnold Schwarzenegger defied this pattern of thought. He believed that sex before or after weight lifting and exercise helped him relax and increased vasodilation, which in turn enabled his practice.

It is true that bodybuilding, especially weight gain, lowers testosterone levels, but still, it only stays slightly lower for less than 3 hours.

Researchers later did tests to measure testosterone levels so as to see what really went on. In studies performed with rats, testosterone levels were tested before ejaculation, immediately after one, two, and then after four. The experiments in rats showed a significant increase in testosterone levels after 1 and remained at the highest level in rats even after 4 ejaculations spanning for about 4 hours.

This shows the great promise that post-ejaculation exercises will naturally be enhanced by increased sexual activity. This is true either with a partner or alone. It seems that these tests are all misleading in one way, but almost all of them are done for men.

Many bodybuilders and athletes fear that sex will hinder the progress of their sport or exercise because it uses a reasonable amount of testosterone. However, this appears more and more to be a myth. In fact, repetitive sex has no negative effect on your weight lifting performance. The effect of sex on your bodybuilding goals may surprise you. In fact, your sex life has a lot to do with the factors that make muscle growth effective. Of your hormone energy levels, sex affects muscle growth more than you think. The following are some of the positive and negative effects of sex on muscle growth.

The Positives

• Testosterone levels

Sex has a positive effect on bodybuilding because it increases testosterone production. Testosterone is a male hormone that promotes a man's primary characteristics such as